T0360438

Strategic Communication for Startups and Entrepreneurs in China

This book presents a comprehensive guide for public relations and strategic communication professionals and entrepreneurs to effectively manage the communication aspects of startups in the context of business in China. Drawing on interdisciplinary theories, current issues, and updated research evidence obtained from entrepreneurs and startup leaders in China, this concise volume provides research-based insights on the best practices for public relations and strategic communication in the unique context of startups. It addresses relationships with stakeholders, public relations practice, leadership communication, and how to leverage the power of social media in the entrepreneurial context.

Strategic Communication for Startups and Entrepreneurs in China will be of great benefit to public relations and strategic communication scholars and practitioners, startup leaders and entrepreneurs interested in opportunities in China, and advanced students in public relations, business communication, and entrepreneurship.

Linjuan Rita Men is an associate professor of public relations at the University of Florida, USA, and chief research editor of the Institute for Public Relations' Organizational Communication Research Center.

Yi Grace Ji is an assistant professor of public relations in the Richard T. Robertson School of Media and Culture at the Virginia Commonwealth University, USA.

Zifei Fay Chen is an assistant professor in the Communication Studies Department at the University of San Francisco, USA.

Routledge Insights in Public Relations Research

The field of PR research has grown exponentially in recent years and academics at all career levels are seeking authoritative publication opportunities for their scholarship. **Routledge Insights in PR Research** is a new program of short-form book publications, presenting key topics across the discipline and their foundation in research. This series will provide a forward-facing global forum for new and emerging research topics which critically evaluate contemporary PR thinking and practice.

This format is particularly effective for introducing new scholarship reflecting the diverse range of research approaches and topics in the field. It is particularly effective for:

- Overview of an emerging area or "hot topic."
- In-depth case-study.
- Tailored research-based information for a practitioner readership.
- Update of a research paper to reflect new findings or wider perspectives.
- Exploration of analytical or theoretical innovations.
- Topical response to current affairs or policy debates.

Authors from practice and the academy will be able to quickly pass on their thinking and findings to fellow PR scholars, researchers, MA and PhD students and informed practitioners.

Strategic Communication for Startups and Entrepreneurs in China
Linjuan Rita Men, Yi Grace Ji, and Zifei Fay Chen

For more information about this series, please visit www.routledge.com/series/RIPRR

Strategic Communication for Startups and Entrepreneurs in China

Linjuan Rita Men, Yi Grace Ji, and Zifei Fay Chen

Routledge
Taylor & Francis Group
LONDON AND NEW YORK

First published 2020
by Routledge
2 Park Square, Milton Park, Abingdon, Oxon OX14 4RN

and by Routledge
52 Vanderbilt Avenue, New York, NY 10017

Routledge is an imprint of the Taylor & Francis Group, an informa business

British Library Cataloguing-in-Publication Data
A catalogue record for this book is available from the British Library

Library of Congress Cataloging-in-Publication Data
Names: Men, Linjuan Rita, author. | Ji, Yi Grace, author. | Chen, Zifei, author.
Title: Strategic communication for startups and entrepreneurs in China / Linjuan Rita Men, Yi Grace Ji and Zifei Fay Chen.
Description: Milton Park, Abingdon, Oxon ; New York : Routledge, 2020. | Series: Routledge insights in public relations research | Includes bibliographical references and index.
Identifiers: LCCN 2019045899 (print) | LCCN 2019045900 (ebook) | ISBN 9780367222840 (hardback) | ISBN 9780429274268 (ebook)
Subjects: LCSH: Business communication—China. | Public relations—China.
Classification: LCC HF5718.2.C6 M46 2020 (print) | LCC HF5718.2.C6 (ebook) | DDC 659.20951—dc23
LC record available at https://lccn.loc.gov/2019045899
LC ebook record available at https://lccn.loc.gov/2019045900

ISBN: 978-0-367-22284-0 (hbk)
ISBN: 978-0-429-27426-8 (ebk)

Typeset in Times New Roman
by Apex CoVantage, LLC

Contents

Acknowledgements

Rita would like to thank her beloved family members, husband Andrew Hu, daughter Aria Hu, mother Li Men, and mother-in-law Li Jiang for their endless support, understanding, and encouragement in the completion of this undertaking. She would also like to thank her friends in the entrepreneurship and investment circle in China, including Zilong Zhao, Jian Fang, Yi Fang, Minjie Qian, and Andy Chen for their help in recruiting interviewees for this project, and former classmates and alumni from the Intensive Training Program of Innovation and Entrepreneurship at Zhejiang University, Jiaju Luo, Jie Mei, Yuan Cheng, and many others for offering help and insights for our studies. She thanks all the interviewed entrepreneurs for their time and support. Lastly, she would also like to extend thanks to the College of Journalism and Communications at the University of Florida for funding support.

Grace would like to thank her hometown Hangzhou and its progressive entrepreneurial scene for the initial inspiration on starting research in entrepreneurship. She would also like to thank her partner Ming and cat Fudge for the support they gave her while writing this book. She would also like to thank all the interviewed entrepreneurs for providing their time and invaluable information. Lastly, she would also like to thank Virginia Commonwealth University for the funding support.

Fay would like to thank her friends and former classmates, Yingru Ji, Yang Yang, Xubin Qin, and many others from the Intensive Training Program of Innovation and Entrepreneurship at Zhejiang University for helping her reach the entrepreneurs in the interview project. She would also like to thank all the interviewed entrepreneurs for their time and support. She would also like to thank the University of San Francisco and its Faculty Development Fund Committee for their funding support.

1 Why startup strategic communication?

Startup companies and new ventures are important to economic growth in the modern society as they help drive innovation, competition, and create employment opportunities. The boom of startup companies and their contribution to the economic development have attracted increasing attention from academic and business communities worldwide. China, a unique and rapidly evolving market, in particular, has witnessed a roaring growth of startup companies in recent years. It is reported that between 2014 to 2018, about 21.6 million companies were registered in China as a result of the government's push for entrepreneurship and innovation to bolster growth (Xinhua, 2018).

Entrepreneurs in China are motivated by the success stories of companies that started from ground zero and finally reached initial public offering (IPO) status in stock markets, both on the mainland and overseas, such as the Alibaba Group, Xiaomi, and Luckin Coffee. According to Yahoo Finance, in 2018, 33 Chinese companies went public in the United States. This number doubled that of 2017, accounting for 17% of all US IPOs (Hu, 2018). In the domestic market, to boost economic growth, the Chinese government has offered both financial and policy supports for startup companies to drive entrepreneurship and innovation. In 2014, China introduced mass entrepreneurship and innovation policies to stimulate mass innovations. Since then, more than 4,200 new hackspace companies have been established. They serve over 120,000 startup businesses and have raised more than RMB 5.5 billion (USD 870 million) (Xinhua, 2018). As a new growth engine for the economy in China, the mass entrepreneurship and innovation policies were further emphasized by China's Premier Li Keqiang at a State Council meeting in 2018. Highlighting innovation as a strategic pillar for a modern economic system, Premier Li addressed that further efforts would be made to upgrade the mass entrepreneurship and innovation policies to broaden the coverage and enhance services and support for business startups and innovation (China.org.cn, 2018).

In educational institutions, entrepreneurship and innovation have also become a popular curriculum and, in some universities, a degree program. Led by Tsinghua University, the Innovation & Entrepreneurship Education Alliance of China was established in 2015. It comprises 137 Chinese universities with research, education, or training emphasizing entrepreneurship. Some of them provide the most prominent entrepreneurial education programs in China, including Peking University, Tsinghua University, Zhejiang University, Shanghai Jiaotong University, and Fudan University. These entrepreneurial education programs have played a significant role in preparing young, talented entrepreneurs in China. For instance, in 1999, Zhejiang University established the Intensive Training Program for Entrepreneurship and Innovation (ITP), China's first intensive training program in entrepreneurial management. It offers a variety of entrepreneurship-related undergraduate courses. Some of the core courses include Entrepreneurial Management, Entrepreneurial Investment and Finance, Technology Innovation Management, New Project Development and Management, and so forth.

Nevertheless, in the curriculum of most entrepreneurship programs, strategic communication courses such as startup public relations, communication management, or corporate communication are currently missing. On the research side, while entrepreneurship scholarship has been growing steadily on a global scale, the topic of startup strategic communication has been underexplored. With an increasing amount of capital and talent entering the new arena of the entrepreneurial economy, there is a lack of guidance for entrepreneurs and venture capital, particularly concerning how to develop effective communication strategies, tactics, and tools to build a startup image, reputation, and manage relationships with various stakeholders. While existing entrepreneurship literature has tackled some related issues such as startup branding, reputation, and internal communication, only recently, the literature overall is scattered with a lack of systematic view of how strategic communication for startups should be practiced.

There are two reasons why we believe knowledge on startup strategic communication should be advanced. First and foremost, strategic communication is crucial for the sustainable growth of a startup business. Strategic communication cannot be separated from any stage of a new venture development. No matter whether the goal is to establish a vision, build a startup brand, or launch and promote products, a startup needs to manage relationships with various stakeholders (e.g., investors, customers, employees, government, media, and the community) and handle issues and crises. Second, although public relations and strategic communication have evolved as disciplines and practices in the past decades, most of the theories and knowledge accumulated are based on research conducted in large corporations. Different from established companies, startups bear many distinctions pertaining to its early developmental stage in the business cycle, company size, structure, and lack of identity and resources. The unique characteristics of startups as compared with large and established corporations require specific guidelines for their strategic communication activities. Obviously, the functions that public relations or strategic communication often serves at large companies, such as branding, reputation management, corporate social responsibility, and marketing communications, may be different for startups. A public relations strategy that works for a multinational company may not be suitable for a startup. Next, we delve into the definition of a startup and its defining characteristics. We also discuss what strategic communication for startups may entail, which leads to an overview of the structure of this book.

Startups: defining characteristics

There exists an extensive body of industry reports and academic literature on startups and new ventures. In the literature, many terminologies are used interchangeably. In addition to startups, they are also referred to as entrepreneurial companies, small businesses, new ventures, and more. Despite the heated discussions surrounding this topic, there has been a lack of consensus regarding how a startup should be defined. Some researchers referred to startups as small companies in the early stage of development with a high-tech focus that create innovative products and services (MacVicar & Throne, 1992). Some described entrepreneurial companies as creating and identifying business opportunities in often ever-changing and fast-moving environments (Sarasvathy, 2001; Shane & Venkataraman, 2000). Others emphasize the size of startups, referring to them as small to medium-sized enterprises (SMEs), and they draw insights primarily from SME research and practice to guide startup operations (Bresciani & Eppler, 2010; Abimbola, 2001; Krake, 2005). In our book, we consolidate the definitions and approaches from these realms and take into consideration the unique cultural and economic background of the recent entrepreneurship development in China (see more in Chapter 2).

We delimit the scope of discussion in this book with a particular focus on Chinese startups that are privately held, innovation and high-tech driven, and fast-growing new businesses dedicated to exploring and building sustainable and scalable business models. Generally, these startups are young, given that their establishment was fewer than ten years ago. They often operate on an internal structure that is similar to SMEs with fewer than 100 employees and valued often at less than RMB 3.35 billion (USD 500 million).

As mentioned earlier, the unique features of startup companies differentiate them from large and established corporations, which consequently calls for tailored strategies for successful business and communication management. The uniqueness of startups is multifold. First, as a growing business, there is no established corporate identity or reputation for a startup (Pet-kova, Rindova, & Gupta, 2008). A company's reputation and image are gained over the years (Fombrun, Gardberg, & Sever, 2000). They are the results of stakeholders' perceptions of a company via long-term interactions and relationship cultivation. Reputation and image are also highly correlated with a company's past performance, which can be unstable during the early stages of the company. A startup company may not possess enough valid performance data to plug into the equation for its reputation.

Second, startups represent companies built from scratch that do not have mature internal structures and processes (Rode & Vallaster, 2005). Due to the shortage of personnel and financial support, in many young firms one employee may play multiple roles concurrently (Abimbola, 2001; Wong & Merrilees, 2005). This is especially true for top leaders and founding members, such as the CEO. It is not uncommon to find a startup CEO performing multiple roles at the same time, including human resources manager, media relations specialist, investor relations liaison, product manager, and sometimes even more. The task distribution within a startup can also be unspecified. For instance, the communication department usually is not a stand-alone unit in a startup. Instead, its functions can be dissolved into multiple departments or served by different people, such as human resources, business development, marketing, and the executive team.

Moreover, startup companies are usually limited in the knowledge support from former market success (Rode & Vallaster, 2005). Many startup companies are not only new in terms of history, but also are exploring new territory that has never been covered by others. As a result, with no prior experience to rely upon, startups make mistakes and learn from them. The positive side of lacking preceding examples is that startups may be presented with limited to no policy constraints or business competitions. In this new "Westland," they have the opportunities to drive without a speed limit and grow exponentially within a short period. Lastly, branding is of great importance for customer acquisition in startups, and the survival and sustainability of the company are primary goals (Boyle, 2003; Mueller, Volery, & Siemens, 2012). This generates a challenge for startups, as they need to invest in building a clear brand vision and image with limited resources.

Strategic communication in startups

Strategic communication is often used to denote an array of communication activities, such as public relations, marketing communication, advertising, and managerial communication. It emphasizes how an organization can advance its mission through the strategic application of intentional communication (Hallahan, Holtzhausen, Van Ruler, Verčič, & Sriramesh,

2007). Coined initially as to how organizations compete in the marketplace to obtain competitive advantage and market share or position (Hatch, 1997), the term *strategic* now has afforded new meanings. For instance, *strategic* communication underscores the communication function that takes on more responsibilities in making managerial decisions as opposed to a focus on technical roles. Strategic communication now is deemed an interdisciplinary concept that advances an organization's mission and its goal/objective achievement through purposeful communication. In the philosophy of organizational *strategic* communication, stakeholders are expected to be engaged and sustain collaborative and mutually beneficial relationships with the organization. As a consequence, stakeholders' knowledge level, attitudes, and behaviors associated with the organization and/or its product and services will likely change in a positive way, favoring the organization (Hallahan et al., 2007). Specifically, in the context of startups, what stakeholders know about, what they are familiar with, and their attitudes and actions toward the startup form the foundation of the startup's return on expectation (ROE) index. The ROE index, comprised of reputation, relationships, trust, credibility, and confidence, can ultimately influence and predict a startup's return on investment (ROI) (Stacks, Dodd, & Men, 2013).

The attention given to startups has stemmed primarily from the perspectives of management and entrepreneurship; however, the aspect of strategic communication or public relations has been largely neglected. Even among the most notable studies, though few, that touched upon communication of startups, the discussions are scattered and peripheral. For instance, two studies that focus on startup branding suggest that startup companies should not force themselves to compare with multinational firms but need to develop more creative and innovative brand communication activities that consider their unique characteristics (Merrilees, 2007; Ojasalo, Natti, & Olkkonen, 2008). Another study that examined startup reputation building suggested that startups could build their local reputation centered around a small group of local stakeholders, whereas symbolic activities and investment in social capital help startups build a generalized reputation (Petkova et al., 2008). In addition, there exist some discussions on creating a startup company identity and personality in the literature. Entrepreneurs are advised to build brand focusing on the role of product attributes and brand personality, and to identify factors that can impact startups' corporate identity, such as vision, aesthetics, play, charisma, and trust (Boyle, 2003; Steiner, 2003). Another study explored particularly pre-IPO startups' internal communication practice and provided a model that covers various aspects of strategic communication. These aspects included employee communications, organizational structure and culture, public relations and communication models, leadership styles, decision-making approaches, employee motivation, and human resources (Saini & Plowman,

2007). Each of the studies mentioned here addressed individual issues or functions of startups' strategic communication/public relations efforts. There is a lack of an overarching and systematic roadmap that can guide startups to navigate in the maze of entrepreneurial communication management.

To address this issue, we launched a multi-phased project that aimed at understanding how strategic communication is and should be practiced in startups in China. The project was initiated in 2015 and included an ongoing literature review on startup strategic communication issues across management, business, and communication disciplines. We conducted in-depth interviews with Chinese entrepreneurs whose startups have achieved recognized success in aspects of strategic communication (stage 1), content analyzed top startups' social media communication profiles (stage 2), and quantitative surveys of startup consumers, social media users, and employees in China (stage 3). This book represents a comprehensive discussion of startup strategic communication that not only draws insights from previously published academic studies, periodical news stories, and industry reports, but also integrates empirical evidence from our 28 in-depth interviews with Chinese entrepreneurs (see Table 1.1 for interviewee background), content analysis of 25 startups social media profiles, and three different surveys with over 2,600 startup employees and consumers.

We structured this book with nine chapters. Following the current chapter, which serves as an introduction to the issue of startup strategic communication, Chapter 2 presents an overview of the historical development and status quo of startups and entrepreneurship in China. The unique political, social, and cultural backgrounds of China and the opportunities and challenges they posed for startup strategic communication practices are also discussed. Chapter 3 takes the stakeholder management perspective, and identifies and analyzes key stakeholder groups and their strategic priorities, particularly for Chinese startups in modern business society. Chapter 4 delves into the functions of public relations in startups. Following the management approach to public relations, the chapter defines public relations, identifies the specific functions along with examples of typical activities, and offers a side-by-side comparison of public relations functions at startups and large corporations. Chapter 5 summarizes both traditional and newly-emerged strategic communications strategies that Chinese startups adopt to cultivate mutually beneficial relationships with various stakeholders. This chapter also concludes the organizational outcomes of building and nurturing favorable relationships with stakeholders for startups. Chapter 6 turns to the internal aspect of startup communication and particularly focuses on the important issue of culture building. Various types of effective startup culture and factors that shape startup culture in China are discussed in detail, leading to a road map for Chinese entrepreneurs on how to build a successful startup culture. Chapter 7 presents a comprehensive examination of entrepreneurial leadership communication that highlights the strategic role of

Table 1.1 Interviewee Background

Interviewee Profiles			Affiliated Startup Profiles			
Entrepreneur	Gender	Title	Year of Establishment	Number of Employees	Financing Status	Company Product or Service
Bin	M	COO	2012	50+	Pre-A	Social networking/dating app
Chao	M	COO	2014	9	N/A	Internet finance
Chun	F	COO	2014	30	A	Designing and selling smart bikes; developing mobile apps for smart bikes
Dan	M	COO	2014	20	Angel	A mobile application to connect photographers and customers
Hang	M	CEO	2014	100+	B	3D interior design technology
Jia	F	PR Manager	2014	120	B	Online photo sharing community
Jian	M	CEO	2010	300+	N/A	Big data based social media marketing and mobile game operation
Jie	M	CEO	2008	300+	N/A	Education services and consulting
Jing	F	Media Relations Manager	2013	24	A	Designing and selling smart bikes; developing mobile apps for smart bikes
Ju	M	COO	2014	80	A	Offering services as personal grocery shoppers
Kang	M	General Manager	2014	17	A	Digital video marketing
Ke	M	CEO	2014	18	N/A	Manufacturer and online retailer of ecological agricultural products
Lei	M	CEO	2012	40	A	A mobile app for cosmetics review; relying on big data to generate industry reports
Liang	M	CEO	2014	7	Angel	Community transportation and ride-sharing services

(*Continued*)

Table 1.1 (Continued)

Interviewee Profiles			Affiliated Startup Profiles			
Entrepreneur	Gender	Title	Year of Establishment	Number of Employees	Financing Status	Company Product or Service
Long	M	CEO	2011	170	N/A	E-commerce for foreign brands
Min	M	CEO	2014	30	A	Designing and selling smart bikes; developing mobile apps for smart bikes
Ping	F	CEO	2014	300+	C	Beauty services booking app
Qin	F	CEO	2014	40+	Pre-A	O2O (online to offline) tailor and wardrobe consulting services
Ran	F	PR Director	2012	50+	Pre-A	Social networking/dating app
Rui	M	Product Manager	2009	80+	N/A	SaaS for hospitals and medical institutions
Wu	M	CEO	2011	50	N/A	Focusing on control products and solutions for fluid machinery
Xiang	M	Chairman of the Board	2006	100+	Strategic investment	Products for people with vision impairment
Yang	M	CEO	2012	50+	Pre-A	Social networking/dating app
Yi	M	CEO	2012	200+	B/Pre IPO	Push notification service for mobile app developers
Yuan	M	CEO	2014	50+	A	Cloud storage for enterprise companies (SaaS)
Yue	M	CEO	2014	15	Angel	Manufacturer and online retailer of ecological agricultural products
Zhan	M	CEO	2014	40+	A	A mobile app for cross-border e-commerce
Zhen	M	Partner and CEO	2014	19	N/A	An investment fund focusing on startup companies

Note: Angel = Angel round, Pre-A = Pre-series A round, A = Series A round, B = Series B round, C = Series C round.

startup leaders as communication agents. Insights are provided on why entrepreneurial leadership communication matters, what purposes it serves, and what communication strategies and channels work. Chapter 8 responds to the prevalent use of social media by both companies and consumers and discusses the unique social media landscape in China and purposes of social media communication for startups. The chapter also provides important guidance for Chinese startups on what communication strategies and tactics to adopt for social media success. Pulling practical insights and implications from each chapter, Chapter 9 synthesizes best practices for effective startup strategic communication. Actionable recommendations are provided for entrepreneurs and communication professionals who work in or for startups in China to effectively practice strategic communication to achieve business objectives.

In sum, strategic communication in the startup and entrepreneurial context is an area of great scholarly and practical importance as startups have distinguishable characteristics that call for more context-specific best practices guidelines. We offer this book as a comprehensive guide for entrepreneurs and strategic communication professionals to understand the current state and development of entrepreneurship in China, effectively design and practice strategic communication, cultivate relationships with stakeholders, perform leadership communication, and leverage the power of social media in the unique context of startup and entrepreneurial communication. Based on our multi-year project on strategic communication in the startup and entrepreneurship context in China, this book draws on interdisciplinary theories, empirical studies, current issues, and cases and examples from entrepreneurs and startup leaders in China to provide rich insights on the best practices for startup strategic communication. This book is intended for a broad audience including strategic communication scholars and practitioners, startup leaders, entrepreneurs, and undergraduate and graduate students majoring in entrepreneurship, strategic communication, public relations, marketing, and business administration. For readers who are interested in international and global communication, this book provides a unique perspective and in-depth understanding of the entrepreneurial dynamics, as well as business and communication environment in modern China.

References

Abimbola, T. (2001). Branding as competitive strategy for demand management in SMEs. *Journal of Research in Marketing and Entrepreneurship, 3*(2), 97–106.

Boyle, E. (2003). A study of entrepreneurial brand building in the manufacturing sector in the UK. *Journal of Product and Brand Management, 12,* 79–93.

Bresciani, S., & Eppler, M. (2010). Brand new ventures? Insights on start-ups' branding practices. *Journal of Product & Brand Management, 19*(5), 356–366.

China.org.cn. (2018, September 7). China to upgrade mass entrepreneurship and innovation. Retrieved from www.china.org.cn/business/2018-09/07/content_62698666.htm

Fombrun, C. J., Gardberg, N. A., & Sever, J. M. (2000). The reputation quotient[SM]: A multi-stakeholder measure of corporate reputation. *Journal of Brand Management, 7*(4), 241–255.

Hallahan, K., Holtzhausen, D. R., Van Ruler, B., Verčič, D., & Sriramesh, K. (2007). Defining strategic communication. *International Journal of Strategic Communication, 1*(1), 3–35.

Hatch, M. J. (1997). *Organization theory: Modern, symbolic, and postmodern perspectives.* Oxford: Oxford University Press.

Hu, K. (2018, December 28). Chinese companies flooded into the U.S. IPO market in 2018. *Yahoo Finance.* Retrieved on August 14, 2019 from https://finance.yahoo.com/news/chinese-companies-flooded-u-ipo-183408925.html

Krake, F. B. G. J. M. (2005). Successful brand management in SMEs: A new theory and practical hints. *Journal of Product and Brand Management, 14*(4), 228–238. doi:10.1108/10610420510609230

MacVicar, D., & Throne, D. (1992). *Managing high-tech start-ups.* Boston, MA: Butterworth-Heinemann.

Merrilees, B. (2007). A theory of brand-led SME new venture development. *Qualitative Market Research: An International Journal, 10*(4), 403–415.

Mueller, S., Volery, T., & Von Siemens, B. (2012). What do entrepreneurs actually do? An observational study of entrepreneurs' everyday behavior in the start-up and growth stages. *Entrepreneurship Theory and Practice, 36*(5), 995–1017.

Ojasalo, J., Natti, S., & Olkkonen, R. (2008). Brand building in software SMEs: An empirical study. *Journal of Product and Brand Management, 17*(2), 92–107.

Petkova, A. P., Rindova, V. P., & Gupta, A. K. (2008). How can new ventures build reputation? An exploratory study. *Corporate Reputation Review, 11*(4), 320–344.

Rode, V., & Vallaster, C. (2005). Corporate branding for start-ups: The crucial role of entrepreneurs. *Corporate Reputation Review, 8*(2), 121–135.

Saini, S., & Plowman, K. (2007). Effective communications in growing pre-IPR start-ups. *Journal of Promotion Management, 13*, 203–232.

Sarasvathy, S. D. (2001). Causation and effectuation: Toward a theoretical shift from economic inevitability to entrepreneurial contingency. *Academy of Management Review, 26*, 243–263.

Shane, S., & Venkataraman, S. (2000). The promise of entrepreneurship as a field of research. *Academy of Management Review, 25*, 217–226.

Stacks, D. W., Dodd, M., & Men, L. R. (2013). Corporate reputation measurement. In C. Carroll (Ed.), *Handbook of communication and corporate reputation* (pp. 561–573). London: Blackwell.

Steiner, L. (2003). Roots of identity in real estate industry. *Corporate Reputation Review, 6*(2), 178–196.

Wong, H. Y., & Merrilees, B. (2005). A brand orientation typology for SMEs: A case research approach. *Journal of Product & Brand Management, 14*, 155–162. doi:10.1108/10610420510601021

Xinhua. (2018, February 10). Over 20 mln new companies registered in China in past 5 years. Retrieved on August 30, 2019 from www.xinhuanet.com/english/2018-02/10/c_136965365.htm

2 The state of startups and entrepreneurship in China

This chapter provides an overview of the state of startups and entrepreneurship in China. It focuses on innovation-based entrepreneurship for a context-based understanding of strategic communication for startups and entrepreneurship in China. First, we briefly recap the development of startups and entrepreneurship in China since the reform and opening-up policies in 1978. We then discuss the opportunities and challenges for startups and entrepreneurs in China from both the social, policy-level perspective (macro level) and the startup perspective (micro level). To further understand the context of this book, we also review the unique business environment, norms, and culture in China. This chapter concludes with implications for the practice of public relations and strategic communication in this specific context.

An overview of the startups and entrepreneurship development in China

The Chinese economy has gone through rapid development since the introduction of the reform and opening-up policies in 1978. The reform and opening-up policies, led by Deng Xiaoping, included a series of initiatives such as the Open Door Policy (opening the country for foreign investment), transitioning from a planned economy to a market economy, and encouraging the growth of the private sector. Over the last four decades, China has grown from one of the poorest countries in Asia to the second-largest economy in the world, with an average annual growth rate of 9.3% in gross domestic product (GDP) (Xi, 2018).

Along with rapid growth in GDP and the private sector is the development of startups and entrepreneurship in China. Since the reform and opening-up policies of 1978, startups and entrepreneurship have evolved in three major phases (Yang & Li, 2008). At the beginning of the market transition (phase I), entrepreneurship relied on personal networks to obtain sources of funding. In the early stage of market transition (phase II), the personal network–oriented structure transformed into a rule-based structure. However, given the transitioning economy, entrepreneurship focused on quantity over quality through cost reduction. As the market transition was gradually completed (phase III), the focus of entrepreneurship has shifted toward innovation. Notwithstanding different models (e.g., network-based, innovation-based, sole trading [*ge ti hu*]) of entrepreneurship in China (Atherton & Newman, 2018), this book focuses on innovation-based startups because they are the current dominant force of entrepreneurship in China.

The status quo

Startups and entrepreneurship in China have grown exponentially in recent years as the government provides policy and financial support to encourage innovation and entrepreneurship. According to the 2019 Global Startup Ecosystem Report by Startup Genome, several cities/regions in China made it to the list of the top 30 global startup ecosystems, ranking second to the United States. Among the top 30 ecosystems, Beijing ranked third, Shanghai ranked eighth, and Hong Kong ranked 25th (Startup Genome, 2019). In addition, Hangzhou and Shenzhen were identified as "challenger startup ecosystems," meaning they are likely to make it to the list in the future based on their current growth. In 2014, 14% of the "unicorns" (i.e., privately held startup companies valued at over USD 1 billion) worldwide were from China; that number increased to 35% by 2018 (Loizos, 2018). Based on the Global Entrepreneurship Monitor entrepreneurial framework conditions as of June 2017, China's physical infrastructure and internal market dynamics obtained 7.2 and 7.1, respectively, on a 9-point scale, followed by entrepreneurial finance (5.5), cultural and social norms (5.3), and entrepreneurial education at post-school stage (5.1) (GEM, 2018). Despite the slowdown of GDP growth in recent years, startups and entrepreneurship are expected to continue playing their vital role in sustaining economic growth, providing jobs, and driving innovation (Pan & Yang, 2019).

Industries

Startups and entrepreneurship are growing in various sectors in China, but the most prominent growth has been witnessed in high-tech sectors that emphasize innovation and technology. To facilitate the economy's transition from low-cost, labor-intensive, and manufacturing-driven economic growth to high-tech and innovation-driven growth, the Chinese government has implemented a series of initiatives. These initiatives have encouraged innovation-based entrepreneurship (Atherton & Newman, 2018), including high-technology zones, tax incentives, and financial support.

As of 2018, the information technology (IT) industry in China attracted most venture capital investments by volume (RMB 37.26 billion [USD 5.41 billion]) (Zero2IPO, 2019a) and by sheer numbers (974 venture capital [VC] investments) (Zero2IPO, 2019b). Immediately following the IT industry are the Internet industry (RMB 32.3 billion [USD 4.69 billion] in volume and 729 VC investments in number) and the biotechnology/pharmaceutical industry (RMB 33.5 billion [USD 4.86 billion] in volume and 677 VC investments in number). Other industries' ranks vary in volume and in number of VC investments but are much lower than IT, biotechnology/ pharmaceutical, and Internet industries. The industries following the aforementioned three in volume are telecommunications sector/value added service (RMB 18.22 billion [USD 2.64 billion]), financial sector (RMB 17.26 billion [USD 2.50 billion]), and automotive sector (RMB 10.1 billion [USD 1.47 billion]). The entertainment and media sector (253 VC investments), telecommunications sector/value added service (241 VC investments), and financial sector (216 VC investments) follow the IT, Internet, and biotechnology/pharmaceutical industries in sheer numbers. The distribution of VC investments is also reflected in what CEOs in China perceive as the top areas to strengthen new business opportunities. In a survey conducted by PwC with 182 CEOs, innovation (19%), competitive advantage (16%), and digital and technological capabilities (13%) were identified as the top three areas (PwC, 2017).

Geographical distributions

Startups in China generally tend to cluster in several metropolitan regions along the east coast, such as Beijing, Shanghai, Hangzhou, and Shenzhen. The government has established these areas as high-technology zones to encourage innovation-based entrepreneurship (Atherton & Newman, 2018). Taking Beijing as an example, the Zhongguancun Science and Technology Zone is a hub for high-tech startups. Many well-known startups, such as Didi Chuxing (a ride-hailing app) and Helijia (a beauty service app), are headquartered in Beijing. Hangzhou is also a booming hub for high-tech startups. The Alibaba Group, headquartered in Hangzhou, has inspired many startups and entrepreneurs. To support entrepreneurship, the local government in Hangzhou has implemented various initiatives, including free office space, tax incentives, and seed funding.

The geographical distribution of startups and entrepreneurship in China is influenced by various factors including financial resources, business networks, and government policy. From a business network view, the clustering of startups may be predicted by localized economies (Guo, He, & Li,

2016). In localized economies, companies from the same industry tend to cluster together, which helps facilitate local linkage with customers, suppliers, labor market, and knowledge spillovers (Guo et al., 2016). Thus localized economies help reduce entry barriers for startups with the accessibility of resources. The clustering of small firms also encourages the development of startups and entrepreneurship because they help link to specialized local suppliers, provide knowledge sharing, and the experience and opportunities to start new businesses. This phenomenon, known as the "Vernon-Chinitz effect" (Chinitz, 1961; Vernon, 1960), was found to positively influence entrepreneurship in China (Guo et al., 2016). Owing to the clustered geographical distribution, acknowledging the disparity of the geographical distribution of startups and entrepreneurship in China is necessary. Hence, the Chinese government launched the "Go West" policy in 1999 to encourage private business and entrepreneurship in the Western region (Atherton & Newman, 2018). Although notable progress has been made, such geographical disparity still exists in today's China.

Characteristics of entrepreneurs in China

The characteristics of entrepreneurs in China have changed over the years. In the early ages of the reform and opening-up (the 1980s), entrepreneurs focused on the manufacturing sector and identified businesses opportunities during the economic transition (Atherton & Newman, 2018). Prominent figures include Zhang Ruimin (Haier Group) and Ren Zhengfei (Huawei). As the Chinese government encouraged privatization and entrepreneurship in the 1990s, entrepreneurs started to explore opportunities in the service industry (Atherton & Newman, 2018). Prominent figures include Li Shufu (Geely Group) and Chen Dongsheng (Taikang Life). As the Internet boomed, entrepreneurs started exploring opportunities in the Internet and technological industries. These entrepreneurs tend to be young and better educated, with many having experience studying or working abroad (Atherton & Newman, 2018). Prominent figures include Robin Li (Baidu) and Ma Huateng (Tencent).

Entrepreneurs today in China are relatively young and well educated. The Global Entrepreneurship Monitor reported that as of June 2018, among the 2,000+ participants surveyed, 10.9% of those who were 18-24 years old reported to be involved in early-stage entrepreneurial activities (i.e. launched businesses that are less than 42 months old or in the process of starting their own businesses). The percentages of adults involved in early-stage entrepreneurial activities are 12% for 25-to 34-years olds, 13.2% for 35- to 44-years olds, 10.8% for 45- to 54-years olds, and 5.1% for 55- to 64-years olds (GEM, 2019). Many entrepreneurs from this young generation were also returnees from overseas with graduate degrees (Atherton & Newman, 2018).

Opportunities and challenges

The unique Chinese sociocultural, economic, and political background and characteristics of startups (see more about the characteristics of startups in Chapter 1) have brought opportunities and challenges for startups and entrepreneurs in China. Next we provide an overview of these opportunities and challenges from the macro- and micro-level perspectives.

Opportunities

At the macro level, startups and entrepreneurs in China enjoy opportunities from policy and economic support as well as growing consumer needs. The Chinese government has been implementing a series of initiatives to support the growth of startups, especially in high-tech industries. In 2010, the Chinese government identified seven strategic emerging industries for which it plans to increase policy support as part of the economic revitalizing measures (US-China Business Council, 2013). These industries include (1) energy-efficient and environmental technologies, (2) next-generation IT, (3) biotechnology, (4) high-end equipment manufacturing, (5) new energy, (6) new materials, and (7) new-energy vehicles (US-China Business Council, 2013). Following this initiative, China's Premier Li Keqiang addressed the notion of mass innovation and entrepreneurship in his speech at the Summer Davos Forum in September 2014 (Fujishiro, 2018). In 2017, the Internet, big data, and artificial intelligence were identified by China's President Xi Jinping as priorities to boost China's global innovation (Statista, 2019). Over the years, many government policies have been implemented to promote innovation and entrepreneurship in China, including support of funding, providing office spaces, and tax reduction. For example, the policies of "mass innovation and entrepreneurship" have helped create a better financial and business environment for startups, with incubators, tax exemption, subsidies for research and development (R&D), and funds to venture capitals (Fujishiro, 2018; Pan & Yang, 2019).

Besides policy support, growing consumer needs also created opportunities for the growth of startups in China. According to the Global Consumer Confidence Survey, the consumer confidence index (a measure to evaluate consumer confidence in employment, personal economic conditions, and willingness to spend) in China has remained high, with 115 points in the second quarter of 2019 compared with the global index of 107 (an index above 100 represents positive, whereas below 100 represents negative) (Nielsen, 2019). The vast adaptation to mobile technology across the country has also provided ease and a viable system for consumer-facing Internet businesses to grow in China.

At the micro level, startups have characteristics that allow them to be daring to take bold action and opportunities. Compared with large corporations, startups are nimble, making them agile in fast-changing environments. Although startups have yet to establish their corporate reputation and culture, such characteristics allow them to cultivate a desirable identity, reputation, and culture right from the start. Moreover, driven by people's need for a higher purpose and value, startups envision an inspiring career growth for potential employees, especially the young generation in China (Tian, Wu, & Wang, 2018).

Challenges

Despite many opportunities for the growth of startups and entrepreneurship in China, several issues pose challenges. At the macro level, the other side of fast development of startups and entrepreneurship is fierce competition. As the number of new ventures and entrants grows in each industry, so does competition. Such competition may sometimes lead to aggressive price-cutting to combat rivals, which consequently leads to reduced profits. Examples include the long-standing price war from 2012 to 2014 between the formerly dominant ride-hailing apps, Didi and Kuaidi, which eventually led to a strategic merger in 2015. Likewise, the fierce price war between bike-sharing startups Mobike and ofo has ensued for years. The aforementioned clustering phenomenon in startups' geographical distribution helps streamline resources. However, clustering may also intensify competition as businesses that provide similar products and services try to win over customers. Moreover, as startups mature and succeed, their business models may also be adopted by new entrants, driving down the profit margin of the original enterprise (Atherton & Newman, 2018). Besides the intense competition that comes with exponential growth, startups and entrepreneurs in China face challenges brought by the dynamic and fast-changing business environment and adoption of new technologies.

At the micro level, startups in China face obstacles brought by the inherent characteristics of startups and new ventures. Compared with large, established corporations, startups are virtually unknown when they first enter the market. Making their companies known remains an essential and challenging task for entrepreneurs. Startups also lack established financial and human resources; hence, having designated personnel for specialized organizational functions is difficult for them. As a result, entrepreneurs and employees in startups usually play multiple roles in their day-to-day jobs, which requires well-rounded skill sets and knowledge.

Doing business in China

The unique sociocultural environment in China requires an understanding of its business norms and practices. The impact of culture on business practices in China is not one-dimensional. Although Chinese philosophies such as Confucianism and Daoism influence the way business people and entrepreneurs operate in China, the recent impact of globalization cannot be neglected (Atherton & Newman, 2018).

Cultural influences

Confucianism is a major philosophical doctrine in China. It was founded by Confucius (about 500 BC) and provides social and behavioral norms for the Chinese throughout history. Confucianism advocates benevolence, harmony, and the "golden rule" (i.e., not treating others the way one would not like to be treated). Confucianism embodies a series of social morality and ethical norms to achieve harmony. Daoism (or sometimes Taoism) is another important philosophical doctrine that was founded by Laozi (about 600 BC). Unlike Confucianism, Daoism values spontaneity and the harmony between human and nature over rigid rules or hierarchy. Business scholars argued that Confucianism and Daoism influence the way people conduct businesses in China (e.g., Atherton & Newman, 2018). For example, influenced by Confucianism, people in China tend to mediate when resolving disputes. The values of hierarchy, familism, and seniority have led to a society with relatively high power distance. Influenced by Daoism, people in China tend to have a positive view toward uncertainties and are adaptive to a fast-changing environment, which result in favorable traits for an entrepreneur.

From a contemporary lens (e.g., Hall, 1989; Hofstede, 2001), Chinese culture can be considered high context; the meanings of messages are conveyed indirectly and need to be interpreted as they relate to the context and the environment. From Hofstede's (n.d.) cultural dimensions, China is identified as high in collectivism (i.e., acting in the interest of groups rather than individuals), high power distance (i.e., unequal distribution of power in organizations), low uncertainty avoidance (i.e., the tendency to avoid ambiguous and unknown situations), high in masculinity (i.e., wanting to be the best rather than pursuing one's preferences), and long-term oriented (i.e., efforts to prepare for the future) (Hofstede Insights, n.d.).

However, considering cultural influences from a static, clear-cut approach is too simple. The trend of globalization has also made Chinese culture integrated with the rest of the world. With increasing exposure to the Western culture, technological interactions, and educational experience overseas, the younger generations in China nowadays become highly influenced by low power distance and individualism. Young entrepreneurs in China are likely to cultivate their startup culture of openness, provide high accessibility for employee participation in decision-making (i.e., low power distance), and incorporate a reward system that recognizes individual contributions (i.e., high individualism) (see more about culture and culture influence in Chapter 6).

The practice of guanxi

Guanxi is a widely acknowledged and studied cultural and social concept in China. Loosely translated as "connections" or "networks," guanxi stems from Confucianism. It values social rules, human interactions, and hierarchical structure and authority (Park & Luo, 2001). In business settings, guanxi is used to obtain access to resources and information (Chen, Chang, & Lee, 2015). Guanxi is also evident when personal connections and relationships are used as assets for organizational purposes (Park & Luo, 2001). Past studies in business and management have shown that good guanxi can lead to positive organizational performance, such as sales and profit growth (e.g., Luo, Huang, & Wang, 2012; Park & Luo, 2001).

For startups and entrepreneurs in China, guanxi is commonly used to develop business and provide a favorable environment for startups to survive and grow (Atherton & Newman, 2018). Positive guanxi with the government can help businesses to obtain regulatory information in a timely manner. Good guanxi with a supplier can help a startup fulfill an urgent order. Guanxi not only facilitates the growth of businesses but also helps to reduce risks and avoid negative consequences. For instance, by establishing good guanxi with government officials, entrepreneurs are able to know about regulatory or policy changes ahead of time, allowing them to be proactive with changes.

Overall, understanding the state of startups and entrepreneurship in China also requires understanding the cultural and business norms there. Although learning about China's traditional cultural values and its national cultural dimensions is important, one should not neglect that globalization and cultural influences from the West have made the business norms in China much more dynamic than before.

In summary, startups and entrepreneurship in China have grown rapidly since the reform and opening-up policies. In the past decade, innovation-based startups have notably become the dominant force of entrepreneurship. The Chinese government has provided substantial policy and financial support for startups and entrepreneurs to grow. Along with the exponential growth and opportunities for startups in China are challenges from the fierce market competition and the inherent characteristics of startups. To establish and implement successful strategic communication programs for startups in China, the status quo, opportunities, and challenges from the socioeconomic perspective, as well as business norms from the cultural perspective, must be understood. Information needs to be regularly updated as policy shifts may impact the development of startups and entrepreneurship. When it comes to culture and business norms in China, one not only needs to consider the traditional values and national cultural dimensions but also the more integrated, dynamic cultural perspectives driven by globalization.

References

Atherton, A. M., & Newman, A. (2018). *Entrepreneurship in China: The emergence of the private sector*. London: Routledge.

Chen, M.-H., Chang, Y.-Y., & Lee, C.-Y. (2015). Creative entrepreneurs' guanxi networks and success: Information and resource. *Journal of Business Research*, *68*, 900–905.

Chinitz, B. (1961). Contrasts in agglomeration: New York and Pittsburgh. *American Economic Review: Papers and Proceedings*, *51*(2), 279–289.

Fujishiro, K. (2018, February). Factors behind rise in startups in China. *Mitsui & Co. Global Strategic Studies Institute Monthly Report*. Retrieved from www.mitsui.com/mgssi/en/report/detail/__icsFiles/afieldfile/2018/04/20/180216i_fujishiro_e.pdf

GEM. (2018a, April 6). Evaluation of China's entrepreneurial environment based on the GEM framework as of June 2017 [Chart]. *Statista*. Retrieved on July 28, 2019 from www.statista.com/statistics/883792/china-entrepreneurial-framework-condition-evaluation/

GEM. (2019, January 21). Percentage of the adult population involved in early-stage entrepreneurial activity in China as of June 2018, by age group [Graph]. *In Statista*. Retrieved November 21, 2019, from https://www.statista.com/statistics/883767/china-early-stage-entrepreneur-population-share-by-age-group/

Guo, Q., He, C., & Li, D. (2016). Entrepreneurship in China: The role of localisation and urbanisation economies. *Urban Studies*, *53*(12), 2584–2606. doi:10.1177/0042098015595598

Hall, E. T. (1989). *Beyond culture*. New York, NY: Doubleday.

Hofstede, G. (2001). *Culture's consequences: Comparing values, behaviors, institutions and organizations*. Thousand Oaks, CA: Sage.

Hofstede Insights. (n.d.). Country comparison: China. Retrieved from www.hofstede-insights.com/country-comparison/china/

Loizos, C. (2018, April 20). Startup ecosystem report: China is rising while the US is waning. *Tech Crunch*. Retrieved from https://techcrunch.com/2018/04/20/startup-ecosystem-report-china-is-rising-while-the-u-s-is-waning/

Luo, Y., Huang, Y., & Wang, S. L. (2012). Guanxi and organizational performance: A meta-analysis. *Management and Organization Review*, *8*(1), 139–172. doi:10.1111/j.1740–8784.2011.00273.x

Nielsen. (2019, July 13). Global consumers remain confident, but improvements less broad-based across markets. *The Conference Board*. Retrieved from www. conference-board.org/data/bcicountry.cfm?cid=15

Pan, F., & Yang, B. (2019). Financial development and the geographies of startup cities: Evidence from China. *Small Business Economics*, *52*(3), 743–758. doi:10.1007/s11187-017-9983-2

Park, S. H., & Luo, Y. (2001). Guanxi and organizational dynamics: Organizational networking in Chinese firms. *Strategic Management Journal*, *22*(5), 455–477. doi:10.1002/smj.167

PwC. (2017, January 12). Top areas to strengthen for new business opportunities according to CEOs in China as of end 2016 [Chart]. *Statista*. Retrieved on July 29, 2019 from www.statista.com/statistics/700576/china-top-areas-to-strengthen-for-new-business-opportunities/

Startup Genome. (2019, May 9). Global startup ecosystem report. *Startup Genome*. Retrieved from https://startupgenome.com/reports/global-startup-ecosystem-report-2019

Statista. (2019, January 16) Startups in China: Statistics & facts. *Statista*. Retrieved from www.statista.com/topics/4769/startups-in-china/

Tian, X., Wu, Y., & Wang, Y. (2018). Career calling of nascent entrepreneurs in China: Structure and measurement. *Social Behavior and Personality: An International Journal*, *46*(4), 695–704. doi:10.2224/sbp.6656

US-China Business Council. (2013, March). China's strategic emerging industries: Policy, implementation, challenges, & recommendations. Retrieved from www. uschina.org/sites/default/files/sei-report.pdf

Vernon, R. (1960). *Metropolis 1985*. Cambridge, MA: Harvard University Press.

Xi, S. (2018, December 6). The future of China's reform and opening-up. *International Policy Digest*. Retrieved from https://intpolicydigest.org/2018/12/17/the-future-of-china-s-reform-and-opening-up/

Yang, J. Y., & Li, J. (2008). The development of entrepreneurship in China. *Asia Pacific Journal of Management*, *25*(2), 335–359.

Zero2IPO. (2019a, February 14). Volume of venture capital investments in China in 2018, by sector (in billion yuan) [Chart]. *Statista*. Retrieved July 29, 2019 from www.statista.com/statistics/234965/volume-of-venture-capital-investments-in-china-by-industry/

Zero2IPO. (2019b, February 14). Number of venture capital investments in China in 2018, by sector [Chart]. *Statista*. Retrieved July 29, 2019 from www.statista.com/statistics/225817/number-of-venture-capital-investments-in-china-by-sector/

3 Understanding the stakeholders of startups

The practice and research of strategic communication and public relations have developed a new emphasis on building and maintaining quality relationships with strategic stakeholders (Kent & Taylor, 2002). Its theoretical foundation dates back to the late 20th century. Researchers borrowed insights from management and interpersonal communication literature and declared that public relations practice and research should focus on relationship building between an organization and its stakeholders (Ferguson, 1984, 2018; Ledingham & Bruning, 1998). Relationships form when stakeholders are affected by consequences created by an organization. This notion acknowledges the importance of strategic stakeholders and their interdependence with different environments, such as economic, social, political, and cultural well-being (Hon & J.E. Grunig, 1999; Ledingham & Bruning, 1998). In this chapter, we explore the strategic stakeholder groups that Chinese startups cultivate relationships with. We also seek to explain why and how startups identify these groups as key stakeholders in the unique contexts of entrepreneurship and cultural, economic, and political environments in China.

What is a stakeholder?

By definition, a *stakeholder* is someone who relates to an organization because of their potential influence on an organization's mission and objectives. Stakeholders are conscious of a mutual relationship with an organization and are interested in the organization and its well-being (Sandman, 2003; Smith, 2017). In many circumstances, stakeholders and *publics* are used interchangeably. However, strictly speaking, the linkage of publics with an organization is primarily established via messages, and not all of them clearly perceive that they have an established relationship with an organization, nor are they concerned about it (Rawlins, 2006).

Another synonym of stakeholder is *market*. Markets' connections with an organization are consequences of marketing efforts, such as purchases, investments, and partnerships. Their relationship with an organization directly impacts the bottom line, particularly its financial success. Markets can be considered a subcategory of stakeholders with specific business foci. At a broad level, *audiences* are the information receivers of a particular medium. They read, watch, or listen either proactively or passively to news from a target organization, but their relationship with the organization is mediated via the medium to which they pay attention. Following this logic, not all audiences are stakeholders. Only the ones who share common interests and values with a target organization and actively seek news about it can be considered stakeholders.

Startups in China acknowledge the critical role of relationship cultivation with their stakeholders. The entrepreneurs we interviewed prioritized the following stakeholder groups: employees, customers, investors, the media, and the government, with the first three being the primary foci. Interviewees also mentioned other stakeholders, including suppliers, retailers, business partners, and competitors. In the next section, we examine each primary stakeholder group and explain why they are crucial to Chinese startups. We also provide suggestions for entrepreneurs who are interested in starting a business in China on how to identify key stakeholders for strategic communication.

Stakeholders of startups in China

Employees

Among all the stakeholder groups, employees are regarded as the most critical for Chinese startups. Undoubtedly, employees are the productive force for a company. Their talents and skills are the core competitive advantage that determines the R&D, product innovation, technological development, and future of startups (Men, Ji, & Chen, 2017). The entrepreneurs that we interviewed remarked that founding team members and early employees can determine "how far the company can go." Innovation and R&D are the cornerstones for startups to survive in the market, and they cannot be achieved without the talents and skills of employees. This is perhaps the reason why many successful companies, such as Google, Tesla, and Pinterest, have loyalty programs that honor employees who joined the company at the earliest stage. These employees are proudly addressed as "No. X" employees. One of the most well-known stories is the first 18 members of the Alibaba Group, known by the moniker "Eighteen Luohan (or Arhats)."

This label acknowledges their dedication and commitment to the company since its early stages.

The second reason why employees are the most essential stakeholders is due to their fundamental contribution and influence on company culture. At the startup stage, the culture of an organization binds people together to pursue its shared value and to achieve organizational goals (Men, Chen, & Ji, 2018; see more about startup culture in Chapter 6). A company's culture is not formed in one day but is a product of long-term cultivation. Although a startup's culture is often determined by the leadership team at its initial stage, its refinement and iterations are influenced by its employees who identify themselves with the company culture and pass it along to newcomers. Yuan, the CEO of a software as a service (SaaS) startup, emphasized that "we need to ensure that the people we recruit fit our culture and possess entrepreneurial spirits." He also remarked that employees hired at the early stage of a startup greatly influence company culture. Organizational culture needs to be acknowledged and upheld by employees. Yuan said:

> From the beginning, it was my co-founders and me who influenced our employees. Now with the expansion of our teams, to ensure the steadiness and efficiency of the operations the senior employees who have synced their values with the company are casting impact to their new colleagues.

Undeniably, one of the biggest challenges for startups is talent recruitment and acquisition. Our research shows that startups in China proactively nurture their relationships with employees. In addition to merit-based rewards, startups invest substantially in team-building and internal communication to ensure that teams work "effectively, steadily, and efficiently," as mentioned by Yue, the CEO of a startup producing and selling ecological agricultural products online. Following their tagline, "a foodie company," and to enhance employees' identification with the company, Yue and his company even built a gourmet kitchen in the office and provide unlimited, imported snacks.

In addition to the critical internal role that employees play as the production force, they serve as ambassadors when facing external stakeholders. They are the intercessory stakeholders who network with other stakeholder groups, such as clients, customers, and media, and nurture the relationships with them on behalf of a company. Yuan highlighted that when customers contact us, their questions need to be handled with care and respect. "Our employees serve as the bridge in keeping good relationships with clients and customers."

Customers

Customers may be the most apparent type of stakeholder because they contribute directly to a company's sales, revenue, and survival. Similar to mature and large corporations, startup companies' customers largely contribute to their financial performance. Customers of innovative and high-tech startups are no longer considered traditional consumer goods shoppers. Instead, they can be users who download application software, people who rent shared bikes, organizations who adopt cloud services, to name a few. Entrepreneurs consider customer acquisition a significant activity of startups due to its capacity in increasing the visibility of new ventures (e.g., McCarthy, Krueger, & Schoenecker, 1990; Mueller, Volery, & Von Siemens, 2012). Take the Internet-based ride-hailing business in China for example. At one point, more than five firms co-existed and provided similar services. The most well-known ones were DiDi, Kuaidi, and You Bu (Uber in China). Although the latter two were merged with DiDi, these three companies initially were in fierce competition to expand their respective customer base. Their common business strategies were running subsidy campaigns and price wars (Kirby, Eby, Frost, & Frost, 2016).

In addition to providing customers direct discounts and financial benefits, entrepreneurs in China consider that product quality positively influences a mutually beneficial relationship. Such relationship further impacts consumer growth and the company's revenue and bottom line. Yi is the CEO of a fast-growing high-tech startup. At the time of the interview, his company was preparing for their IPO. He shared, "A company cannot survive without a continuing relationship with its customers. That's why we emphasize the 'knee-down' service and treat our customers with the highest respect." Lei, the CEO from a cosmetic product review and retailing company, also values their consumers and remarked:

> They are an essential group among all our stakeholders. We care tremendously about their benefits and how they perceive us. The app we provide is the biggest one in the cosmetics category. Users who download and use our app are our consumers. We have to make sure we offer them the best user experiences. We ensure them the reviews (about cosmetics products) on our app are objective and credible.

Similar to employees, customers serve as intercessory stakeholders. On social media, customers can become opinion leaders who steer people's perception of a startup and its products. Such communication activity, known as electronic word-of-mouth, is a double-edged sword that can positively or negatively impact a startup's image. Our interviewees specified that word-of-mouth and third-party endorsements are more trustworthy channels than advertising, especially in a collectivist society such as China, in which publics rely heavily on social networks and personal connections for information (Men & Tsai, 2012; Wang & Wei, 2012). Through a survey of more than 600 Chinese customers, we found strong correlations between perceived relationship satisfaction and positive advocacy behavior toward startups. Results indicate that when customers truly enjoy their interactions and business encounters with a startup, they would have a strong tendency to recommend this company and its products to family and friends, repurchase their products, act as the company's voluntary ambassadors, and even defend the company when it is criticized.

Investors

The third group of primary stakeholders is investors. Entrepreneurs recognize the importance of maintaining a favorable relationship with investors, who not only provide financial support but also various resources. With the boom of China's venture capital and fierce competition among investment funds, entrepreneurs and startups are reasonably empowered in their relationship with investors (Fannin, 2015; Men et al., 2017). Thus startup companies keep their investors updated and informed while capitalizing on the funds, resources, and connections they provide despite the absence of daily interactions with them. The frequency and purpose of interactions between a startup and its investors are considerably distinctive from those with employees and customers.

Among the participating startups in our interviews, only three did not raise money from investment funds or individual investors. Regardless, almost every entrepreneur we talked to had encounters with investors. A healthy startup-investor relationship can yield several positive outcomes. Zhan, the CEO of an e-commerce startup, agreed: "Investors are here to support us. Besides money, they can bring in helpful resources. They also assist us in recruiting top talents in the field to fill in core positions, maintaining key client relationships, and developing new business endeavors." Yuan, the CEO of a software as a service (SaaS) startup, categorizes the assistance they receive from investors into twofold. First, tangible values include "money and the connections they build for us with key resources, clients, and more connections." The other type of assistance is intangible values:

> For instance, our investor is the top notch in China. Having them invested in us is like having a strong endorsement. It will impact our future rounds of fundraising and even talent recruitment. Besides, because our investor has invested in many startups, they share great experiences with us that help us tremendously in our development.

From the other end of the spectrum, Zhen, the partner and CEO of an investment agency, remarked:

> We respect every decision they (startups we invested in) made, their company culture, and the strategy they look to implement on their blueprint. I even think we should give them more autonomy. Companies make mistakes, yet they learn from their mistakes. The more mistakes they make during their early years, the faster they will take off later.

The media

The media is also recognized as an essential stakeholder. The media landscape in China has dramatically changed over the past decade because of technological advancements (Men & Tsai, 2012; see more in Chapter 8). As a result, media relations have also evolved. Departing from traditional media such as newspapers, trade magazines, television, and radio, digital media has emerged and has attracted enormous attention among startups. We-media and grassroots media are the two emerging media groups frequently mentioned by entrepreneurs. These channels are possessed and created by startups or online influencers on the basis of established social media platforms such as Sina Weibo and WeChat. Results from our content analysis with 25 Chinese startup companies revealed the vast majority had active Weibo and/or WeChat accounts. Chinese startups use social media for a variety of reasons, including dissemination of company information, promotion and mobilization, general (non-company) news sharing, thought leadership, social listening, customer service, and dialogue. They are proficient in using social media and take advantage of the apps' features, such as incorporating different message styles, vividness features (using emojis, pictures, videos, etc.), and functional interactivities, when composing messages. Another type of new media is digital news publishers that concentrate on covering technological and innovative industrial news (e.g., *36 Ke, Hu Xiu Net, Tai Media*, and *B-12* in the high-tech industry; Chen, Ji, & Men, 2017). The contents published on them are filtered and edited by news editors through the gatekeeping process. This process often takes longer than announcing news on social media. Readers can find detailed and insightful information, including technology news, analysis of emerging trends, profiles of new businesses and products, and financial funding updates.

An increasing number of startups adopt social media as they provide a vast amount of innovative cost-effective branding opportunities and business benefits with wide reach (Bresciani & Eppler, 2010; Lingelbach, Patino, & Pitta, 2012). Engaging in social media helps startup companies achieve branding objectives and attract customers and employees. The interviewees indicated that startups generally favored the We-media, the influential industry media, and individual celebrities and opinion leaders ("Big V") over traditional official media outlets because of their objectivity and unparalleled influence on digital publics. Lei, the CEO of a cosmetics product review and online retailing company, commented:

> It's not that we don't want to make a placement with traditional media even if we have the money. It is primarily because their cost efficiency is relatively low. In general, you need to budget 50 million to 100 million RMB for that. We are not at that stage yet to purchase placements in traditional media.

Others also found the fast-changing social media landscape a challenge. "WeChat has already surpassed Weibo, and you just can't predict what the future will be," said Lei.

Although most startup companies recognize the benefit of using media for obtaining free publicity, generating awareness, and attaining organizational legitimacy, some were concerned about the risk of overexposure to the public. Dan, the COO of an online photography startup shared: "I personally believe that drawing considerable media attention is disadvantageous for startups, especially when you are yet to develop your technology barrier and core strength. A company will also not benefit from extensively exposing itself to its competitors." In fact, a few startups achieve media success that outpaces their progress in product development, which ultimately leads to business failure. The most infamous story is probably Theranos, a USD 9 billion biotech company based in Silicon Valley that intended to develop a blood-testing system. Its CEO, Elizabeth Holmes, chased high-profile media outlets, such as *TED Talks*, the *New Yorker*, and *Fortune*, and produced viral online videos even before the company produced an effective product as publicized (Zacharakis & Jno-Charles, 2017; Carreyrou, 2015). Researchers advised entrepreneurs that the best time to promote a company is after a major milestone is achieved (Zacharakis & Jno-Charles, 2017).

The government

Unlike the strategic communication practices of multinational companies in China, in which government relations are often challenging (Luo, 2000), startups commonly maintain a "simple" relationship with the government. As discussed in Chapter 2, such a link is developed possibly because of the currently benign, welcoming, and encouraging supportive environment for high-tech entrepreneurship in China. The government encourages startups by providing them with a considerable amount of funding and policy support, especially to those that belong to the high value-added fields (e.g., R&D, high-tech, and biotech) promoted by the government (Fernandez & Underwood, 2009).

The interviewees were clearly divided on the role of the government. IT startups claimed that they do not frequently deal with the government. However, these startups admitted that they capitalize on supportive local government policies for new innovative ventures. Moreover, entrepreneurs with outstanding overseas study or work experiences (*hai gui*) often receive supports, such as tax reduction, free offices, and million renminbi startup funds. In contrast, startups in public health, education, transportation, and agriculture consider government relations a priority. These sectors are traditionally controlled and heavily regulated by the government and require licenses and certification from the government. Rui, the CEO of a SaaS for hospitals and medical institutions startups, said: "When we are certified by the government, it gives us significant credentials and competitive advantage over our competitors. The certification allows the hospitals (our customers) to see that we are trusted by the government – this is incomparable credibility." At the same time, startups equipped with cutting-edge technological skills also partner with the government to meet their needs for a win-win relationship. Yuan, whose startup also provides SaaS services, added: "Because of the uniqueness of our products, we have been working with the local government on standardization, qualification, and data security."

The government does not always serve as an enabler to startups. It can also be a limiter, depending on which industry a startup is in and what specific business it operates. Recent years have witnessed an explosion of online video streaming platforms. By the end of 2017, these platforms were reported to have had more than 42,209 million users (China Internet Network Information Center, 2019). Such platforms generate revenues via advertisements, user contribution, and partnerships with game companies. Statista predicted that China's video live stream market would grow from USD 9.62 billion (RMB 67.62 billion) in 2018 to USD 15.93 billion (RMB 112.09 billion) in 2020 (Statista, 2018). New issues emerge as businesses grow in this industry. To attract attention and stimulate fiscal spending from users, livestream hosts would post inappropriate content, such as nudity and violence. However, some startup companies that provide livestreaming services did not intervene. To regulate this industry and offer citizens a healthy Internet environment, the State Internet Information Office issued a series of provisions on the admonitions of livestreaming services and closed down 18 platforms in 2017 that violated these provisions (Xinhua, 2017).

If the government's regulatory intervention is legitimate as it aims to ultimately improve the online space for Internet users, then its limiter's conduct will appear controversial in the following scenario. Due to unique political and social circumstances, the media in China operate under strict government censorship. The same regulations applied to prevent unhealthy online streaming content are adopted to monitor emerging news media posts. The leaders of news and information content platform startups can be invited by the government for "a cup of tea" if the digital publishers or platforms appear "leftist" or "objective" and do not stop the circulation of anti-government and anti-mainstream ideology contents. The terms "tea-sipping" (喝茶) or "check water meter" (查水表) are euphemisms for police and government interrogation (Zeng, Huang, & Liu, 2018). An anonymous source revealed that those who handle government relations in content publishing startups are constantly under the dilemma of complying with government regulations and professional ethics.

This chapter provides an overview of the key stakeholders that startup companies in China interact with via strategic communication activities. In strategic communication, a "general" stakeholder is nonexistent. Most organizations today have a diverse set of stakeholders, and so do startups in China. Although we identify five major stakeholder groups, we do not claim that each share equal weight. Some are considered more vital than others depending on a startup's industry, development stage, and business focus. With limited financial and personnel resources, a startup cannot maintain satisfactory relationships with every group. To achieve the best outcomes, entrepreneurs and strategic communication professionals need to set their priorities.

To begin with, a startup must conduct an organizational audit and fully understand its strengths, weaknesses, opportunities, and threats while keeping its current and long-term goals and objectives in mind. It should also map out the major stakeholder groups and analyze each of their characteristics, including their interests and needs, how they impact the firm and vice versa, and what their communication patterns are. By comparing the organizational needs with stakeholders' characteristics, the best matches will emerge. Moreover, the position, relationship valence, and relationship strength that a stakeholder group shares with a startup are not static. External stakeholders, such as investors, may evolve into internal players. The government, an enabler that provides startups with policy and financial support, can also be a limiter to digital news publishing startups. Traditional media, which is considered less efficient on ROI by a startup in its angel round of financial funding, may become important when a startup prepares for IPO. To identify key stakeholders strategically, startups need to continually monitor and evaluate their organizational status, stakeholder characteristics, and external environmental changes.

References

Bresciani, S., & Eppler, M. (2010). Brand new ventures? Insights on start-ups' branding practices. *Journal of Product & Brand Management, 19*(5), 356–366.

Carreyrou, J. (2015, October 10). Hot startup Theranos has struggled with its blood-test technology. *Wall Street Journal.* Retrieved from www.wsj.com/articles/theranos-has-struggled-with-blood-tests-1444881901

Chen, Z. F., Ji, Y. G., & Men, L. R. (2017). Strategic use of social media for stakeholder engagement in startup companies in China. *International Journal of Strategic Communication, 11*(3), 244–267.

China Internet Network Information Center. (2019). Statistical report on China's Internet development. Retrieved on August 3, 2019 from www.cac.gov.cn/2019-02/28/c_1124175677.htm

Fannin, R. (2015, September 12). China's VC boom and bust and then what for 2015? *Forbes.* Retrieved from www.forbes.com/sites/rebeccafannin/2015/09/12/chinas-vc-boom-and-bust-and-then-what-for-2015/2/

Ferguson, M. A. (1984, August). Building theory in public relations: Interorganizational relationships as a public relations paradigm. Paper presented to the Association for Education in Journalism and Mass Communication, Gainesville, FL.

Ferguson, M. A. (2018). Building theory in public relations: Interorganizational relationships as a public relations paradigm. *Journal of Public Relations Research, 30*(4), 164–178.

Fernandez, J. A., & Underwood, L. (2009). *China entrepreneur: Voices of experience from 40 international business pioneers.* Hoboken, NJ: John Wiley.

Hon, L. C., & Grunig, J. E. (1999). *Guidelines for measuring relationships in public relations.* Gainesville, FL: The Institute for Public Relations, Commission on PR Measurement and Evaluation.

Kent, M. L., & Taylor, M. (2002). Toward a dialogic theory of public relations. *Public Relations Review, 28*(1), 21–37.

Kirby, W. C., Eby, J. W., Frost, S. L., & Frost, A. K. (2016). Uber in China: Driving in the gray zone. *Harvard Business School Case*, 316–135.

Ledingham, J. A., & Bruning, S. D. (1998). Relationship management in public relations: Dimensions of an organization-public relationship. *Public Relations Review, 24*, 55–65.

Lingelbach, D., Patino, A., & Pitta, D. A. (2012). The emergence of marketing in millennial new ventures. *Journal of Consumer Marketing, 29*(2), 136–145.

Luo, Y. (2000). *How to enter China: Choices and lessons.* Ann Arbor, MI: University of Michigan Press.

McCarthy, A. M., Krueger, D. A., & Schoenecker, T. S. (1990). Changes in the time allocation patterns of entrepreneurs. *Entrepreneurship Theory and Practice, 15*(2), 7–18.

Men, L. R., Chen, Z. F., & Ji, Y. G. (2018). Walking the talk: An exploratory examination of executive leadership communication at startups in China. *Journal of Public Relations Research, 30*(1–2), 35–56.

Men, L. R., Ji, Y. G., & Chen, Z. F. (2017). Dialogues with entrepreneurs in China: How start-up companies cultivate relationships with strategic publics. *Journal of Public Relations Research, 29*(2–3), 90–113.

Men, L. R., & Tsai, W. S. (2012). How companies cultivate relationships with publics on social network sites: Evidence from China and the United States. *Public Relations Review*, *38*, 723–730.

Rawlins, B. L. (2006). *Prioritizing stakeholders for public relations*. New York, NY: Institute for Public Relations Research.

Sandman, P. (2003). Stakeholders. Retrieved on August 3, 2019 from http://psand man.com/col/stakeh.htm

Smith, R. D. (2017). *Strategic planning for public relations*. London: Routledge.

Statista. (2018, June). Market size of online live streaming in China from 2016 to 2020. Statista. Retrieved on Novembers 25, 2019 from https://www.statista.com/statistics/874591/china-online-live-streaming-market-size/

Wang, X., Yu, C., & Wei, Y. (2012). Social media peer communication and impacts on purchase intentions: A consumer socialization framework. *Journal of Interactive Marketing*, *26*(4), 198–208.

Xinhua, (2017, April 2). China shuts down 18 illegal live streaming apps. Retrieved from www.xinhuanet.com/english/2017-04/02/c_136178399.htm

Zacharakis, A., & Jno-Charles, A. (2017). Why Startups shouldn't chase media buzz. *Harvard Business Review*. Retrieved on August 3, 2019 from https://hbr.org/2017/06/why-startups-shouldnt-chase-media-buzz

Zeng, F., Huang, V. G., & Liu, L. (2018). The virtual organization of social movement entrepreneurs: The Internet and new forms of protest in contemporary Chinese society. In J. L. Qiu (Ed.), *Media and society in networked China*. Leiden: Brill.

4　The functions of public relations in startups

With structures, processes, and corporate identity and reputation that are yet to be established, startups need public relations and communication strategies tailored toward these unique characteristics. Many practitioners argue that the focus of public relations efforts for startups should be different from established corporations (e.g., Cohen, 2017; Corbett, 2019). However, with a variety of information available, startups may be overwhelmed to create public relations strategies that are suitable for their companies. To develop effective public relations strategies, we first need to understand what public relations entails. Following the management function approach, public relations practices discussed in this book encompass beyond publicity and promotions. They include a variety of functions that enable the cultivation of relationships with various internal and external stakeholders. We start by reviewing the definition of public relations and the role it plays in organizations. Given the specific sociocultural context in China, we also briefly discuss public relations practices in China. We then delve into the functions of public relations and strategic communication in startups, compare these functions between startups and large, established corporations, and provide suggestions for startups and entrepreneurs to establish effective strategic communication practices.

What is public relations?

Public relations, a central practice of strategic communication, has various textbook definitions. In this book, we adopt the following widely used definition of public relations by Cutlip, Center, and Broom (1994):

> Public relations is the management function that identifies, establishes, and maintains mutually beneficial relationships between an organization and the various publics on whom its success or failure depends.

This definition resonates with other frequently used definitions of public relations. For example, J. E. Grunig and Hunt (1984) define public relations as "the management of communication between an organization and its publics." The Public Relations Society of America (PRSA) (n.d.) defines public relations as "a strategic communication process that builds mutually beneficial relationships between an organization and its publics." These definitions emphasize the strategic management, communication, and relationship building functions of public relations and the interdependence between an organization and its stakeholders.

Public relations plays important roles for various organizations and is essential to organizational effectiveness. Through the cultivation of relationships with stakeholders, public relations brings tangible (e.g., monetary gains) and intangible (e.g., crisis prevention, organizational reputation, brand loyalty) values for organizations (L.A. Grunig, J.E. Grunig, & Dozier, 2002; see more about the value of relationship cultivation in Chapter 5). More importantly, effective public relations practices help organizations understand the interests of diverse stakeholders. In this way, organizations are able to align the interests of organizations and stakeholders and integrate them into organizational behavior to not only contribute to the bottom line, but also to the sustainable development of organizations (Bowen, Rawlins, & Martin, 2010). For example, Cargill is a US company that specializes in food, agriculture, financial, and industrial products and services. It created its Indonesian Palm Oil Sustainability Program to incorporate the interests not only of its customers but also of non-government organizations, suppliers, smallholders, policymakers, and the communities where its businesses operate in. Although the program does not directly generate revenues for Cargill, it helps the company address the interests of various stakeholders and prevents reputational and financial risks (Chen, Stacks, Ji, & Yook, 2017). Although resources are limited for startups, considering the interests from various stakeholders and thinking about long-term success are also important for them. Various interests may be incorporated in the development of products and services. For instance, Ge Tui is a technology company in China, which has recently gone public. Ge Tui provides data intelligence solutions and push notification services. It developed a "heat map" using big data to visualize and predict crowd density. This product helped local communities avoid stampedes and aided the government's disaster relief and crisis communication efforts.

Public relations in China

Along with the growing economy in China, the public relations industry in China has experienced notable development over the years (Ovaitt, 2011). The unique sociocultural conditions in China call for an examination on the public relations practices in the country. A survey with 118 public relations practitioners in China found that they identify with four functions of public relations (Li, Cropp, Sims, & Jin, 2012): (1) As a promotion facilitator, their duties involve production of audio and video materials, event planning, community relations, and social activities; (2) as a public information specialist, their duties entail employee communications, client services, customer relations, and handling public enquiries; (3) as a media relations counsel, their duties include handling media enquiries, crisis management, media training, and hosting press conferences; (4) and as a conflict management expert, public relations practitioners act as intermediaries between an organization and stakeholders. However, access to top management and decision-making remains a challenge for the profession, and such access also varies depending on the different practice areas.

The functions of public relations in startups

The general functions of public relations encompass a wide range of responsibilities and activities, including corporate communication, media relations, investor relations, issues management, employee relations, community relations, donor relations, strategic philanthropy, marketing communication, public affairs, and government relations (Broom & Sha, 2013; Heath, 2005). In practice, these functions may either be stand-alone or fall under certain departments, and the needs for these functions vary depending on organization types and dynamics (Heath, 2005).

The unique characteristics of startups warrant a thorough examination of public relations functions that are tailored for these traits. Unlike large, established corporations, startups are usually in the stage in which their corporate identity, reputation, internal structures, and processes are yet to be established (Petkova, Rindova, & Gupta, 2008; Rode & Vallaster, 2005). They also bear the challenges brought by limited human and financial resources and the lack of knowledge support from previous market experiences (Abimbola, 2001; Rode & Vallaster, 2005). Our research shows that startups have unique needs of public relations functions. Note that the prioritization of the following functions may vary depending on the business models and dynamics for different startups.

Branding and marketing communication

One of the core functions of public relations in startups is branding and marketing communication. At the beginning of the business stage, startups need to establish their brands and generate awareness among stakeholders. As noted by Yuan, the CEO of an enterprise cloud storage company:

> The most important part (of our public relations effort) is branding and educating the market. The knowledge of our product in China right now is still in a relatively early stage. Our customers and prospects do not have much

awareness of cloud storage yet. We will need a plan to educate the market in the long term. At the same time, we also need to build a trustworthy brand.

Ant Financial, now an established digital payment and financial technology firm affiliated with Alibaba, is a success story in market education at its early stage. Ten years ago, consumers were unfamiliar with digital payments. Through sustained efforts in market education, people have come to understand the value and the safety of such technology, which is now seamlessly integrated into the daily lives of the Chinese.

For startups, branding and marketing communication efforts are usually integrated in business operations that are directly tied to the business bottom line. Startups are usually focused on the survival of businesses. According to Zhan, the CEO of a mobile app for cross-border e-commerce, "managing a business is about managing a brand, both internally and externally. We need to effectively operate the market resources to help grow our brand. For me, this is part of business operations."

Owing to limited resources, branding and marketing communication may entail a different focus in the daily operations of startups compared with large, established companies. Startups need to employ creative, innovative, and cost-effective branding and marketing communication strategies to address their needs (Boyle, 2003; Merrilees, 2007). Hence, word-of-mouth marketing becomes extremely important as startups build their brand and try to enter and survive in the market. Kang, the CEO of a digital video marketing company, expressed how endorsement and positive word-of-mouth are crucial for his startup's businesses: "Effective public relations for us is to generate endorsement. In the digital space, that means commenting and sharing to generate more buzz."

Although traditional promotion and media relations are also functions of public relations, they may be given less priority in startups depending on their stage of development. Many of the entrepreneurs we interviewed mentioned that they usually do not have the money to invest in paid media unless it is directly related to their business survival. Publicity in media is something that is "nice to have" rather than a "must have" in their current business stage. Jie, the CEO of an educational services and consulting company, commented:

> Publicity in the media can really generate a lot of eyeballs, and it would be very cost-effective for a company. I will consider taking more advantage of media relations in the future, but right now our business does not have the direct need yet.

Establishing corporate identity, reputation, and image

Given that reputation is predicted by a company's performance history (Fombrun, Gardberg, & Sever, 2000), a startup has no established reputation when it is created. Undoubtedly, reputation management is an important public relations function. However, for startups, this function focuses on establishing and initiating a reputable identity than building and enhancing reputation. A company's reputation involves different dimensions, including products and services, emotional appeal, vision and leadership, financial performance, workplace environment, and social responsibility (Harris Insights & Analytics, 2018). For startups, establishing a reputation requires internal and external public relations efforts. Ran, the public relations manager at a social networking and dating app startup, remarked that "public relations need to be approached from two aspects. One is more internal oriented, and from there, we take an 'inside-out' approach and look at external stakeholders."

For startups, establishing corporate identity, reputation, and image requires different efforts. Ping, the CEO of a beauty services booking app, noted, "Public relations from the internal perspective is to clearly tell the employees what our dreams are. For them, they are helping the beauty service providers find clients." Such efforts help set a clear vision for employees and create a culture that espouses a sense of responsibility (for more about building an effective culture, see Chapter 6). Xiang, the chairman of the board of a company specializing in vision aid products, noted that because their products are highly technical and specialized, communicating with their customers (primarily doctors and hospitals) about their technology and investment in R&D is important for them. Essentially, public relations is about building a professional, expert image and reputation of the company so that more people will get to know the company in a positive light.

Public relations plays a key role in aligning the interests of an organization and its stakeholders. For startups, the needs and interests from stakeholders are often yet to be explored. Therefore, the function of establishing corporate reputation is about informing/educating stakeholders about a company and ensuring that the perceived corporate reputation is aligned with what the company intends to communicate. Ju, the COO of a personal grocery shopping services app, commented, "You have the image of the company in your mind. However, to realize such an image, you need to let people understand it the same way you do. I think that process is part of public relations."

Issues management

Internal and external challenges require startups to spend a significant amount of time on environmental scanning (Mueller, Volery, & Von Siemens, 2012). Owing to their small business scale and limited knowledge, startups may not worry about large-scale crises as much as large corporations do. However, startups are not immune to crises or risks. If the original brand and company knowledge of a startup are associated with negative word-of-mouth or media coverage, then this knowledge would become detrimental for the fundamental survival of the company. Therefore, issues management is a crucial component of public relations functions for startups.

Issues management helps organizations to anticipate threats, minimize risks, and avoid potential crises. It should be a proactive, systematic process that includes the following steps: (1) identification of the issue, (2) analysis of the issue, (3) formulation of strategy options, (4) development of action plans, and (5) evaluation of the results (Wilcox, Cameron, & Reber, 2015). Owing to the limited human and financial resources of startups, a readily available issues management action plan is even more critical. Specific issues may vary depending on a startup's products, services, and industry. The entrepreneurs we interviewed identified various priority issues for their company. For example, a cloud storage service provider focused on cybersecurity issues. A dating app and social networking company identified scamming as a trigger to a potential crisis. Providers of food services listed food safety as the number one issue. Issues management is notably a process that requires collaboration from top leadership with personnel who undertake various functions within a company, including technology, business operations, customer service, and so on. In this way, startups will be able to develop a streamlined process. For example, one of the entrepreneurs from the food industry we interviewed shared a case on how he coped with a food quality issue. The incident occurred during the rainy season in Southeast China. His company shipped packages of pasture-raised organic eggs to customers. The eggs were fresh at the time of the shipment, but they soon started growing molds due to the weather. He received complaints from customers, and some thought the eggs had been stored for months. Although the circumstance was unintentional, he acknowledged the situation and refunded the customers. He commented, "In the age of social media, you really can't bear the loss from negative word-of-mouth, especially when it's related to your core business and corporate identity. It can be fatal for the company."

Relationship building and cultivation

Relationships are the centerpiece in the practice of public relations. For startups, relationship building and cultivation with key stakeholders should be integrated into their daily business operations. The first step in relationship building and cultivation is to identify and prioritize key stakeholders.

Startups' key stakeholders typically include employees, customers, investors, the government, media, and their community (see more details about each key stakeholder in Chapter 3). After identifying and prioritizing key stakeholders, startups should incorporate appropriate strategies to build, cultivate, and enhance the relationships with these stakeholders (for specific relationship cultivation strategies, see Chapter 5). What follows is a brief description on what relationship cultivation with each key stakeholder may entail.

Employee relations

Employees are the bare bones of startups, and cultivating desirable employee relations takes much more than just the efforts from human resources personnel. Entrepreneurs and startups leaders play essential roles in employee relations. Such positions not only include monetary return and rewards but also building a positive startup culture (see more in Chapter 6) and effective leadership communication (see more in Chapter 7).

Customer relations

Regardless of whether a company has a business-to-business or business-to-consumer focus, customers are directly linked to the business bottom line of startups. Customer relations are often directly tied to startups' business operations. In addition to mediated communication via traditional and digital media channels, customer relations are also cultivated via interpersonal communication. This responsibility can be presumed by sales, business development, and customer service personnel. Many of the entrepreneurs we interviewed also noted that positive customer relations led to favorable government and investor relations, as the value of the company is directly connected with the quality of products and services they can provide for their customers.

Government relations

The priority of government relations may differ by the industry that a startup operates in. In China, the government provides supportive policies (e.g., offering incubation systems and providing startup funds and tax reduction) for startups to develop innovative technologies. For traditional industries (e.g., agriculture, education, transportation), obtaining certification and license from government agencies is essential for their business operations. Startups, therefore, need to present their social contributions to obtain policy support. The responsibilities of cultivating government relations usually fall onto the shoulders of entrepreneurs as they carry the corporate and brand identity of their companies.

Investor relations

Investors are essential in raising money for many startups, especially those in high-tech industries, whose products and services have high demands on costs but are slow in returns. In addition to financial support, investors provide other valuable resources for startups' market expansion and talent acquisition. Entrepreneurs are directly involved in the tasks related to investor relationship cultivation, such as regular reporting and participation in investors' events. Investors mostly take a "hands-off" approach to give autonomy to the companies they invest in. However, keeping investors updated with the growth of the company is important in cultivating positive investor relations, leading to win-win relationships between startups and investors.

Media relations

From the information sharing perspective, a good relationship with the media is important for organizations to effectively communicate their messages to other stakeholders in a credible, trustworthy way. For startups, the function of media relations is frequently integrated into brand and reputation building activities. Depending on company size, startups may have one or two employees who focus on external relations activities, including media relations. Entrepreneurs and startup leaders are also often involved in the process; as representatives of their companies, they are usually the ones who provide quotes in media interviews. Rather than focusing on generating coverage with the general public, media relations activities for startups tend to focus on industry-specialized media outlets, such as *36 Ke, Hu Xiu Net*, and *B-12*. However, the coverage and publicity of startups' activities in the media should be aligned with the corporate culture and business operations. Media relations should not be merely regarded as "show work."

A note on the differences of public relations functions between startups and large corporations

As reviewed earlier, the functions and relationship cultivation with stakeholders may share similarities between startups and large, established corporations. However, specific activities, prioritization, and the scope of these functions vary between startups and large corporations. Here we summarize three key differences:

- *The primary purpose of public relations activities for startups is survival compared with maintaining and enhancing corporate and brand image for large corporations.* The branding, marketing communication, and reputation management purpose of startups is mainly to initiate and establish identity, image, and reputation.
- *Public relations functions in startups require more innovative, cost-friendly activities than large corporations.* Owing to financial constraints, startups usually do not have a large budget for advertising and event planning. To achieve their business and organizational goals, startups focus on organic word-of-mouth communication and rely on creative messages and collaboration with well-known companies and brands to boost their image and generate positive feedback from stakeholders.
- *Although large corporations have established public relations and marketing departments, startups often have only a few people who specialize in this area. Thus, public relations in startups requires direct input and involvement from entrepreneurs and their top leaders.* This involvement makes public relations activities inherent in the daily business operations of startups.

Conclusion: effective public relations practices in startups

Based on the understanding of public relations as a strategic management function, this chapter provides a summary and review of the public relations functions for startups and discusses their differences from large, established corporations. We also offer the following theory-based (e.g., J. E. Grunig & Hunt, 1984; Bowen et al., 2010) and evidence-based (Men, Ji, & Chen, 2017) suggestions for startups to practice public relations effectively:

- Instilling public relations into the strategic management process and business operations;
- Involving the entrepreneurs and the top leaders of startups in public relations activities;
- Performing public relations functions with a systematic, integrated approach;
- Being strategic rather than technical;

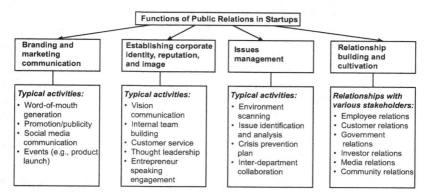

Figure 4.1 Functions of Public Relations in Startups

- Integrating public relations into startups' mission, vision, values, and corporate culture;
- Listening and cultivating long-term relationships with stakeholders;
- Setting clear roles and responsibilities for each function.

Figure 4.1 lays out the functions and activities discussed in this chapter. To establish effective public relations practices, startups need to approach public relations functions in a clear, systematic manner, and integrate public relations into the management process. In the next chapter, we will delve further into the relationship building and cultivation functions and provide strategies that help build positive, mutually beneficial relationships between startups and their stakeholders.

References

Abimbola, T. (2001). Branding as competitive strategy for demand management in SMEs. *Journal of Research in Marketing and Entrepreneurship, 3*(2), 97–106. doi:10.1108/14715200180001480

Bowen, S.A., Rawlins, B., & Martin, T. (2010). *An overview of the public relations function.* New York, NY: Business Expert Press.

Boyle, E. (2003). A study of entrepreneurial brand building in the manufacturing sector in the UK. *Journal of Product and Brand Management, 12*, 79–93. doi:10.1108/10610420310469779

Broom, G.M., & Sha, B. (2013). *Cutlip and Center's effective public relations* (11th ed.). Boston, MA: Pearson.

Chen, Z. F., Stacks, D. W., Ji, Y. G., & Yook, B. R. (2017). Cargill's Indonesian palm oil sustainability program. In J. V. Turk & J. Valin (Eds.), *Public relations case studies from around the world* (2nd ed., pp. 35–52). New York, NY: Peter Lang.

Cohen, I. (2017, January). What startups should do differently when it comes to PR. *Entrepreneur*. Retrieved from www.entrepreneur.com/article/288325

Corbett, C. (2019, January). Guide to public relations for startups: How to hit a PR home run. *Crunchbase*. Retrieved from https://about.crunchbase.com/blog/guide-public-relations-startups/

Cutlip, S. M., Center, A. H., & Broom, G. M. (1994). *Effective public relations* (7th ed.). Upper Saddle River, NJ: Pearson.

Fombrun, C. J., Gardberg, N. A., & Sever, J. M. (2000). The reputation quotient[SM]: A multi-stakeholder measure of corporate reputation. *Journal of Brand Management*, 7(4), 241–255. doi:10.1057/bm.2000.10

Grunig, J. E., & Hunt, T. (1984). *Managing public relations*. New York, NY: Holt, Rinehart and Winston.

Grunig, L. A., Grunig, J. E., & Dozier, D. M. (2002). *Excellent public relations and effective organizations: A study of communication management in three countries*. Mahwah, NJ: Lawrence Erlbaum Associates.

Harris Insights & Analytics. (2018, March). The 2018 Harris poll Reputation Quotient® summary report. *The Harris Poll*. Retrieved from https://theharrispoll.com/wp-content/uploads/2018/12/2018-HARRIS-POLL-RQ_2-Summary-Report_FNL.pdf

Heath, R. L. (2005). Functions of public relations. In R. L. Heath (Ed.), *Encyclopedia of public relations* (pp. 350–353). Thousand Oaks, CA: Sage.

Li, C., Cropp, F., Sims, W., & Jin, Y. (2012). Perceived professional standards and roles of public relations in China: Through the lens of Chinese public relations practitioners. *Public Relations Review*, 38, 704–710.

Men, L. R., Ji, Y. G., & Chen, Z. F. (2017). Dialogues with entrepreneurs in China: How start-up companies cultivate relationships with strategic publics. *Journal of Public Relations Research*, 29, 90–113. doi:10.1080/1062726X.2017.1329736

Merrilees, B. (2007). A theory of brand-led SME new venture development. *Qualitative Market Research: An International Journal*, 10(4), 403–415. doi:10.1108/13522750710819739

Mueller, S., Volery, T., & Von Siemens, B. (2012). What do entrepreneurs actually do? An observational study of entrepreneurs' everyday behavior in the start-up and growth stages. *Entrepreneurship Theory and Practice*, 36(5), 995–1017. doi:10.1111/etap.2012.36.issue-5

Ovaitt, F. E. (2011, December). China and public relations research. *Institute for Public Relations*. Retrieved from https://instituteforpr.org/china-and-public-relations-research/

Petkova, A. P., Rindova, V. P., & Gupta, A. K. (2008). How can new ventures build reputation? An exploratory study. *Corporate Reputation Review*, 11(4), 320–344. doi:10.1057/crr.2008.27

Public Relations Society of America. (n.d.). About public relations. Retrieved from www.prsa.org/all-about-pr/

Rode, V., & Vallaster, C. (2005). Corporate branding for start-ups: The crucial role of entrepreneurs. *Corporate Reputation Review, 8*(2), 121–135. doi:10.1057/palgrave. crr.1540244

Wilcox, D.L., Cameron, G.T., & Reber, B.H. (2015). *Public relations strategies and tactics* (11th ed.). Upper Saddle River, NJ: Pearson.

5 Cultivating stakeholder relationships for startups

In this chapter, we focus on how startups in China build and maintain relationships with their stakeholders. We first discuss how relationship management strategies (e.g., openness, listening, networking, personal relationships, and positivity) from the public relations literature are practiced by Chinese startup companies. Next, we discuss four unique strategies that newly emerged from our data collected from the Chinese startup companies (i.e., vision/value communication, authentic communication, empowerment, and proactive reporting). This chapter concludes with a summary of outcomes of building and nurturing favorable relationships with stakeholders for startups. We hope to present entrepreneurs a comprehensive guide map in effectively building and managing relationships with various stakeholders.

Before we delve into the specific strategies that startup companies in China practice, let us first understand the theoretical origins of relationship management of organizations. As any other social entities, such as individual human beings, organizations need to build and maintain positive relationships with other organizations or individuals they encounter daily. In general, the outcomes of such healthy relationships will benefit not only the organizations but also their stakeholders and the society at large. Toward this purpose, researchers coined six strategies drawing from the interpersonal relationship management literature: *access*, *positivity*, *openness*, *assurance*, *networking*, and *sharing of tasks* (e.g., Hon & J.E. Grunig, 1999; Huang, 2001). Among them, access strategy emphasizes that organizations and their stakeholders should provide easy access to each other. Positivity is that both organizations and stakeholders are committed to making their relationships more enjoyable. Openness strategy intends to guide both entities to show the willingness to engage in direct and open communication. Assurance refers to a positive state that both parties show they are committed to maintaining the relationship. Networking is the strategy that organizations build networks with groups which their stakeholders affiliate and identify with. The sharing of tasks strategy emphasizes collaboration between the organization and their stakeholders in problem solving.

Admittedly, the operation of an organization is not always smooth sailing. Organizations face unexpected turbulences when conflicts and risks occur. Based on the conflict management literature, researchers proposed more relationship cultivation strategies to assist organizations in combating conflicts and lessening damages. The most effective and constructive ones in a long-term relationship building that help to balance the interests of an organization with its stakeholders are *cooperating, being unconditionally supportive*, and *saying win-win or no deal* (J.E. Grunig & Huang, 2000; Hon & J.E. Grunig, 1999). To elaborate, when adopting the cooperating strategy, organizations need to work closely with stakeholders to reach a mutually beneficial relationship. In extreme circumstances, organizations should be unconditionally supportive that they do everything they think is best for the relationship, even if their stakeholders do not appreciate it. Facing conflicts, an organization should prioritize a win-win (i.e., mutually beneficial) relational outcome; they should instead not commit to an agreement that only favors one party. In addition, some other new strategies emerged from different perspectives of relationship studies. For instance, Kelly (1998) introduced the construct of stewardship to fundraising with four strategies: *reciprocity, responsibility, reporting*, and *relationship nurturing*. Although initially developed as associated with nonprofit organizations, these strategies are generally applicable to other types of organizations including startups. Given that a high number of startups are venture capital–backed or are in need of fundraising, managing relationship with investors (see Chapter 3 for more) is an essential practice of strategic communication. Moreover, addressing relationship management from an internal perspective, Rhee (2004) and Kim and Rhee (2006) added *visible leadership, listening, responsiveness, continued dialogue/patience, respects*, and *face-to-face communication* to the list of relationship cultivation strategies with employees to nurture positive employee outcomes. More recently, with the prevalent adoption of social media, *authenticity* has emerged as a novel and critical approach in contemporary communication management (Molleda & Roberts, 2008).

We will stop throwing in terminologies here. Compared with large and established companies, startups have unique characteristics that require their strategic communication practices to adhere to particular guidelines. Keep in mind that the strategies we mentioned earlier were developed mainly based on research in large corporations and thus may not always work effectively in a startup setting. Further, a startup very likely will not end up using all of them in their daily practices. Some of them are more suitable for a particular circumstance; some are more effective in managing certain types of relationships; and some can reach more desirable outcomes when paired with specific communication channels. To present the most comprehensive operation manual, we draw insights from theories of organization-public relationships (OPRs) and indicators and value of quality relationships, taking into consideration specific Chinese culture characteristics, such as relationship orientation, collectivism, and characteristics of startups. We aim to provide theory- and context-based guidance for Chinese startups and entrepreneurs to build win-win and long-term relationships with strategic stakeholders.

Relationship cultivation strategies for startups in China

It is noteworthy that although startups usually have unique strategic communication needs and limited resources, some of the strategies (as presented next) they utilize for relationship cultivation are similar to those used by large corporations (Bresciani & Eppler, 2010; Men, Ji, & Chen, 2017).

Openness/access

Openness/access strategy intends to guide both organizations and their stakeholders to show the willingness to engage in direct communication. By doing so, both entities should create and provide access to each other to engage in open dialogue. Particularly, in the context of startups, companies tend to adopt this strategy for managing employee relations. Many entrepreneurs told us that they emphasized the importance of having an open and transparent culture and a flat organizational structure. Such practice is not common in traditional Chinese organizations. Large and mature Chinese companies often carry the characteristics of high power distance, multiple hierarchies, and power inequality (Hofstede & Hofstede, 2005). Our interviewees told us that many startups in China adopt a "Silicon Valley style." For leadership teams, such as CEOs and co-founders, instead of occupying a separate office, they often share an open workspace with employees. Yi, the CEO of a data-service startup that provides push notification service for mobile app developers, mentioned, "We have an open work environment, and we promote direct and equal communications. . . . During our 'Monday Boss Blah Blah Blah' time, our employees can talk freely with anyone in our management team and ask any questions." Min's company designs and sells smart bikes and cycling apps. As a product manager-type CEO, he also spends an extraordinary amount of time writing codes and debugging with the engineering team. Min told us:

> We always fight; we communicate in a very straightforward way. This is how engineers and geeks communicate. Fundamentally, we don't

actually hate each other, yet we work very cohesively. We share this same goal that is to solve the problem and build the best products.

Positivity

Positivity is another major relationship strategy that startups employ. To build a positive and enjoyable relationship, both parties in the relationship need to act joyfully, be polite, and avoid criticism of the other party (Canary & Stafford, 1992). Quite a few interviewees noted the importance of keeping the relationships enjoyable, content, and fun for employees. According to Yue, the CEO of an startup that produces and sells ecological agriculture products, "Starting a company is like hosting a potluck. Everyone brings your own dishes, join us, and have fun. My long-term goal to let everyone feel enjoyable and happy working together." As a PR manager of a startup that produces an online photo-sharing app and community, Jia highly spoke of her CEO as to how she made an effort to create a positive work environment: "People say we work at an extremely high pace. I actually don't feel it at all. Even if we are working overtime, the entire atmosphere is always enjoyable." Jia told us she had a female CEO and loved having flowers in their office: "Hydrangeas, lilies, roses, even lotus, you name it! She has her own way to spread positive energy among us." Another tactic that Jia's company practices to create and maintain positive relationships both internally and externally is the usage of encouraging and positive language with a joyful twist or "love" words. "For example, we say 'sure *la*,' 'OK *ya*,' 'super cute *la*.'[1] You may find them a bit childish, but they convey our friendly and joyful characters."

Sharing of tasks

Organizations also collaborate with their stakeholders to solve problems concerning either or both of two parties' interests. This is referred to as sharing of tasks (Hon & J.E. Grunig, 1999). For example, China has the most substantial disparities in urban and rural areas regarding income and development. Closing the gaps has been one of the priorities on the Chinese government's economic blueprint for the society for decades. The e-commerce business that Taobao.com operates has helped revitalize rural Chinese villages, home to half the country's population. According to the World Bank, for those villages that broadly engage in e-commerce with Taobao, their transaction volume is estimated with at least RMB 10 million (approximately USD 1.4 million) for every 100 active online shops. The number of *Taobao villages* has increased from 20 in 2003 to 3,202 in 2018 (Luo, 2018). Although not all startups in China keep close ties with the government, as mentioned earlier in this book (see Chapter 3), it does not constrain them from participating to resolve community issues as part of their sharing of tasks strategy. The startup that creates an online photo-sharing app and community, where Jia works as a PR manager, actively involves in philanthropy initiatives. Specifically, they devote themselves to causes related to cleft lip and palate issues. Jia said:

> We don't simply donate money to them or write a social media post about them. Our CEO participated in fundraising and visited several surgical sites. We also used our platforms to conduct a cause-related marketing campaign. We invited artists to our offline event selling their works, the income of which was directly transferred to the Smile Train, China.

Besides sharing of tasks in resolving community and society issues, other business-oriented collaborations also feature task sharing strategy, such as co-branding. The startups we interviewed collaborate with large, established organizations or other startups via both social media and offline events. Yue, the CEO of an ecological food manufacturing startup, shared his stories of co-branding with You Bu (Uber China) and Anmanfayu (an Aman hotel in Hangzhou). Yue's company ended up getting greater exposure as a result of co-branding with companies/brands that had an established image and reputation and a solid fan base.

Saying win-win or no deal

Applying this strategy, all parties in a relationship are beneficiaries. They search out common or complementary interests and solve problems together through open discussion and joint decision-making (Hon & J.E. Grunig, 1999). Ensuring win-win (i.e., saying win-win or no deal) is also considered essentially strategic in startup relationship building because most stakeholder relationships in the early stage are still committed or mutual beneficial. There-fore, common interests help bound startups and their stakeholders together. On the contrary, if startups and stakeholders cannot find a solution that ben-efits both sides, they should agree not to engage and then to make a decision, given the outcome of which is not beneficial for either party in the long run. Ping, the CEO of an Internet-based beauty services startup, explained:

> We have to maintain a win-win relationship with our stakeholders. We co-exist and develop. We try to create an ecosystem in which every species (stakeholder) can live and nurture the soil for growth. This is the only way that we can develop a long-term relationship with our stakeholders.

The case we discussed earlier that Yue's company collaborated with You Bu (Uber China, merged with DiDi in 2016) is also a prominent example of the win-win approach. By the time Uber entered the Chinese market, it was an established brand for their US-based stakeholders. However, for Chinese consumers, it was a newcomer, competing with fast-growing, local ride-hailing services such as Didi and Kuaidi. Through collaboration with a Chinese native startup, You Bu was able to localize their brand and perceived as more friendly and accessible to Chinese users, thus substantially growing their customer foundation.

Listening

Listening is not merely equivalent to paying attention or being attentive. The core of listening is being responsive. Opinions of stakeholders should be brought to the organization, and the organization responds in a timely fashion (Kim & Rhee, 2006; Rhee, 2004). Traditionally, listening is most commonly adopted strategy for managing internal relationships. In the context of startup communication, companies also utilize listening to nurture relationships with customers. Long, the CEO of an e-commerce startup based in Hangzhou, explained:

> You have to understand them (your customers). If you don't "date" with your customers, it's hard for you to understand them truly. Then, it's impossible for you to develop a product that meets their real needs and wants. Not understanding the customers simply means failure. When I was doing the infant clothing business, I followed over 200 pregnant women on Sina Microblog. I read their posts every day and find what are on their mind.

Jia's company builds a photo-sharing app and it is important to create and manage online communities. They particularly adopt listening aided with social media-based communication monitoring. Jia said:

> We have separate operation teams for Weibo and WeChat. They monitor . . . what types of engagement each of them achieved in terms of sharing, viewing, and comments. By doing that we can understand the interests and preferences of our users. We then will enhance what they like about our product and change the things they don't. This is how we make the iteration of our products. We don't want to do a hard sell of our products to users. Instead, we want them to cherish their experience with us from the bottom of their hearts.

Personal relationships

Despite rising expectations for individual freedom, achievement, and individuality, China is still a relationship-oriented collectivist society that values reciprocity, personal connections, and exchange of face and favor (see more about guanxi in Chapter 2). Therefore, personal relationships is another primary relationship cultivation strategy used in the Chinese context. It is particularly essential and useful when cultivating relationships with government officers, investors, and customers. Entrepreneurs we interviewed told us to grow and maintain personal relationships; they often attend industry or government events and activities to make their voice heard. Some startups are proactive by hosting "BBQs, cocktail parties, and small gatherings for networking," said Kang, president of a video content marketing startup. Ke, the CEO of an agriculture product startup, also recalled:

> We reached out to the government through unofficial channels, personal relationships. Once we got connected, we studied their local policies and developed our application materials accordingly. It just gives you more confidence if you have personal relationships with anyone in the government.

If the previously mentioned strategies share much similarities with how established and mature companies build stakeholder relations, in the next section we turn to several new relationship cultivation strategies specifically for Chinese startups that emerged from our interview and survey data, such as vision/value communication, authentic communication, empowerment, and reporting.

Vision/value communication

Vision/value (or in Chinese, 情怀), appeared to be an essential aspect of startup relationship cultivation in China. It is a sound investment for startups as it unites and motivates employees and gives stakeholders a higher shared purpose that transcends individual interests (Men et al., 2017). Having an audacious goal that reflects the startup's societal intelligence also establishes the startup's socially responsible image, contributing to public trust and satisfaction (Mayfield, Mayfield, & Sharbrough III, 2015). For example, Liang, the CEO of a community transportation and ride-sharing startup, mentioned in our interview:

> You need to convince them (the stakeholders) that what we are doing is something meaningful and great. It's not only about making money;

we are creating values for society. For individuals, they would not only get the monetary return, but it is also more about self-development and realizing personal values.

Jia, the public relations manager of a photo-sharing social networking site (SNS), agreed and said:

> The ultimate purpose we develop this photo-sharing social network is not just to make money or become a Fortune company someday. We hope to open a window for everyone and offer a platform for people to share their talents and joy.

Authentic communication

Authenticity has been advocated as a novel communication model for building a lasting relationship with strategic stakeholders (Molleda & Roberts, 2008). From our interviews, many entrepreneurs believed that authentic, honest, genuine, and consistent communication builds stakeholder trust and quality relationships over time. Several CEOs or executive leaders told us based on their experiences that the best and easiest way of communication is being authentic. Jia mentioned to us that her CEO at a photo-sharing SNS startup often told them not to lie: "Only when you tell the truth, you are able to be consistent with all the media outlets and all the parties." Lei, the CEO from a cosmetic product review and online retailing company also shared: "We don't purchase advertorial or place non-reputable cosmetic products in our app to expand our user base. Our practice is entirely based on authenticity and objectivity."

Empowerment

Empowering stakeholders via conversations, collaborations, and decision-making process is another effective strategy for relationship cultivation. Research shows that one of the determinations for employees to join a startup is their recognition of ideas and opportunities to participate in decision-making that lead to beneficial outcomes (Bresciani & Eppler, 2010). When employees are empowered, they generally express more trust, satisfaction, and commitment to the company. Zhan, the CEO of an investment fund, elaborated:

> A lot of decision-making in our company is bottom-up. . . . We want employees to participate, and we give them enough autonomy. As a top manager, I position myself as a service provider. I want my followers

to see me as a resource for them, whom they want to go to when facing problems or need help.

A similar principle holds for customers. Entrepreneurs also revealed that when customers notice that their feedback is valued and addressed by the startup, they would appreciate the company's care and reciprocate with more trust in the startup. As a result, their relationship with and loyalty toward the company are strengthened.

Proactive reporting

Startups use reporting principle to keep investors informed, updated, and in the loop, which helps maintain a healthy and quality investor relationship. Our data from entrepreneurs in China confirmed the effectiveness of this strategy in maintaining relationships with various stakeholders of startups. Hang, the CEO of a 3D home design startup, said, "You have to communicate with the investors proactively and periodically to keep them updated and informed." Guo, the COO of an online photography startup, also shared:

> In our communication with investors, we keep very high level of transparency. We had to completely change our direction of our business and had a board meeting with them and explained why and what would be the next steps. Our investors were very understanding.

Now that we have discussed what communication strategies that startup companies can adopt in building and nurturing good relationships with stakeholders. Next, we turn to the question of how startups in China can benefit from such good stakeholder relations.

Value of stakeholder relationships for startups

Traditionally, *trust, satisfaction, commitment,* and *control mutuality* (*shared control*) are the most commonly measured variables when assessing an organization's relationship outcomes (Huang, 1997). Trust indicates the level of confidence and willingness parties have to be open and vulnerable to one another. Satisfaction reflects the level of favorable feelings. Commitment exhibits the degree to which the relationship is considered worth maintaining and promoting (Hon & J.E. Grunig, 1999). Control mutuality refers to the extent to which parties agree on shared power and influence. In fact, these four relational outcomes basically represent how Chinese entrepreneurs defined positive relationships with stakeholders based on our research.

Overall, the interviewees agreed that good relationships are indicated by various outcomes of *mutual trust, satisfaction, commitment, understanding, cooperation, authenticity*, and most importantly, a *win-win mindset*. For example, elaborating trust and authenticity, Qin, the CEO of an O2O (online to offline) tailor and wardrobe consulting startup, said:

> I think an important indicator (of a good relationship) is whether they tell you the truth and share honest opinions with you. If the customer like your service, they would say so; if they don't think you are good enough, they will provide honest suggestions for you to improve. If people are faking it, I think the relationship is very terrible already.

Explaining a win-win relationship that all the parties benefit from it, Liang, the CEO of a community transportation startup, said:

> Eventually, everyone wins. We succeed as a business as we increase revenue. Our customers benefit because they would have an easier, more economical, and convenient ride to work. For the government and the society, (they win as) we help promote using clean and new energy, reduce emissions, and protect the environment.

Value of startup-stakeholder relationships

Chinese entrepreneurs recognized the importance of relationships with stakeholders for the startup's success and practice relationship cultivation at various levels. Quality organization-stakeholder relationships save money and make money for the organization (L.A. Grunig, J.E. Grunig, & Dozier, 2002). As strategic resources that are valuable, rare, inimitable, and non-substitutable for the organization (Men, 2012), stakeholder relationships build the organization's sustainable competitive advantage and eventually contribute to the attainment of organizational goals and effectiveness (L.A. Grunig et al., 2002).

For Chinese startups, quality relationships are perceived as invaluable capital. Maintaining healthy relationships with their key stakeholders inevitably brings favorable impacts on their bottom lines. There was a consensus among Chinese entrepreneurs that good relationships could contribute to the return on investment of the startup. Yue, the CEO of an ecological food manufacturing startup, stated, "Relationships are the resources and soil for sales and revenue. If you don't have the soil, there will be only short-term benefits." More specifically, positive investor relations could help raise money for the startup. Favorable customer relations could directly boost sales and revenue. Healthy government relations could save startup money through tax reduction, free facilities, and startup funds. Rui, the CEO of a SaaS for hospitals startups, shared:

> Our software helps to set up the standard for monitoring and evaluation in the field. We received full support from the National Health and Family Planning Commission of China. We are testing it now. Once it is approved it will be used nationwide, meaning that we will have more than one thousand clients because they have to follow government regulations.

When it comes to intangible values, interviewees provided various examples regarding how relationships contribute to the startup's success in an invisible way. For instance, quality relationships with employees increases employee loyalty, commitment, identification with the organization, and engagement. Good media relations gives a startup more visibility, free publicity, legitimacy, and credibility, and helps build the brand. Jia, the PR manager of an online photo-sharing app and community, said:

> Tech news media and We-media are more influential among all types of media outlets. Once we are publicized in these two types of media, we will receive spotlights in other media channels as well. It also helps with our publicity and relationship management in the near future, reaching a much bigger radiance converge.

Interviewees also recognized that quality relationships with customers and consumers generate invaluable word-of-mouth and brand endorsement and advocacy. Yang, the CEO of a startup that designs social networking/dating apps, told us their customers are their potential endorsers and ambassadors: "What we say about our own products won't matter as much as what the customers say. Such word-of-mouth is intangible but critical assets for the company." Yuan is CEO of another SaaS startup that operates on a business-to-business model. He concurred, as a B-to-B businesses they do not rely heavily on advertising and large scope marketing. Instead, word-of-mouth in the industry is critical for them to grow, maintaining old clients and gaining new business. "Word-of-mouth is formed based on quality relationships," said Yuan.

This chapter provides strategic insights for strategic communication professionals, startup leaders and entrepreneurs why stakeholder relationships are critical for startups and most importantly, how to build lasting and win-win relationships with different stakeholder groups for startups in China. Various theory-based and data informed strategies are discussed, including fostering openness, positivity, sharing of tasks, saying win-win or no deal, listening, using personal relationships, vision/value communication, authentic communication, empowering stakeholders, and proactive reporting. While this might not be an exhaustive list of strategies that work for Chinese startups' relationship building purposes, and yet specific circumstances, contexts, and stakeholder characteristics need to be considered when using these strategies, this list may serve as an initial checklist for Chinese startups' relationship building efforts.

Note

1 *La, ya, ba,* and *wa* are examples of sentence-final particles in Chinese. They can be found in both Mandarin and Cantonese languages. These types of words are often (not always) used in everyday conversations at the end of sentences. In specific contexts, they carry connotations of joy, cuteness, and innocence.

References

Bresciani, S., & Eppler, M. (2010). Brand new ventures? Insights on start-ups' branding practices. *Journal of Product & Brand Management, 19*(5), 356–366.

Canary, D. J., & Stafford, L. (1992). Relational maintenance strategies and equity in marriage. *Communication Monographs, 59,* 243–267.

Grunig, J. E., & Huang, Y. H. (2000). From organizational effectiveness to relationship indicators: Antecedents of relationships, public relations strategies, and relationship outcomes. In J. A. Ledingham & S. D. Bruning (Eds.), *Public relations as relationship management: A relational approach to the study and practice of public relations* (pp. 23–54). Mahwah, NJ: Lawrence Erlbaum Associates.

Grunig, L. A., Grunig, J. E., & Dozier, D. (2002). *Excellent public relations and effective organizations: A study of communication management in three countries.* Mahwah, NJ: Lawrence Erlbaum Associates.

Hofstede, G., & Hofstede, G. J. (2005). *Cultures and organizations: Software of the mind.* New York, NY: McGraw-Hill.

Hon, L. C., & Grunig, J. E. (1999). *Guidelines for measuring relationships in public relations.* Gainesville, FL: The Institute for Public Relations, Commission on PR Measurement and Evaluation.

Huang, Y. H. (1997). *Public relations strategies, relational outcomes, and conflict management strategies.* Unpublished doctoral dissertation, University of Maryland, College Park.

Huang, Y. H. (2001). OPRA: A cross-cultural, multiple-item scale for measuring organization – Public relationships. *Journal of Public Relations Research, 13,* 61–90.

Kelly, K. S. (1998). *Effective fund-raising management.* Mahwah, NJ: Lawrence Erlbaum Associates.

Kim, H. S., & Rhee, Y. (2006). Exploring relationship cultivation strategies in community relations. Paper presented at the annual meeting of the International Communication Association, Dresden International Congress Centre, Dresden, Germany.

Luo, X. (2018). In China's Taobo villages, e-commerce is one way to bring new jobs and business opportunities to rural areas. *World Bank Blogs*. Retrieved from https://blogs.worldbank.org/eastasiapacific/china-s-taobao-villages-e-commerce-one-way-bring-new-jobs-and-business-opportunities-rural-areas

Mayfield, J., Mayfield, M., & Sharbrough III, W. C. (2015). Strategic vision and values in top leaders' communications: Motivating language at a higher level. *International Journal of Business Communication, 52*(1), 97–121.

Men, L. R. (2012). Revisiting the continuum of types of organization-public relationships: From a resource-based view. *Public Relations Journal, 6*(1), 1–19.

Men, L. R., Ji, Y. G., & Chen, Z. F. (2017). Dialogues with entrepreneurs in China: How start-up companies cultivate relationships with strategic publics. *Journal of Public Relations Research, 29*(2–3), 90–113.

Molleda, J., & Roberts, M. (2008). The value of authenticity in global strategic communication: The new Juan Valdez campaign. *International Journal of Strategic Communication, 2*, 154–174.

Rhee, Y. (2004). *The employee-public-organization chain in relationship management: A case study of a government organization*. Unpublished doctoral dissertation, University of Maryland, College Park.

6 Building an effective startup culture

Culture is an important differentiator of modern organizations. In the startup stage of an organization, in particular, when a brand has not yet been established, culture helps unite people, bind people, and drive people toward the same goal and future and attracts, retains, and motivates talents (Men, Chen, & Ji, 2017). Culture can be linked to the success indicators of performance and productivity for a business. According to a meta-analysis conducted on the relationship between entrepreneurial orientation and business performance, cultural dimensions of innovativeness, risk-taking, and proactiveness are important contributors to the financial and non-financial performance of an organization (Rauch, Wiklund, Lumpkin, & Frese, 2009). In this chapter, we delve into the topic of startup culture and discuss the definition of culture, various types of culture that are effective for startup growth and development, factors that influence the startup culture, and as how to create a culture that is aligned with startup goals in China.

What is culture?

Culture is generally a set of values, beliefs, assumptions, and symbols that determine how organizational members think and behave (Sriramesh, J. E. Grunig, & Buffington, 1992). It answers the questions of who we are (e.g., identity), what we believe in (e.g., values), where we are going (e.g., vision), why we exist (e.g., mission and purposes), and how we are distinct/ unique in the marketplace (e.g., character). Culture is often seen as the foundation of organizational decisions, communications, and actions (Sriramesh et al., 1992). Cultural norms define what is encouraged or discouraged and accepted or rejected within an organization or group (Groysberg, Lee, Price, & Cheng, 2018).

Groysberg et al. (2018) further identified four core attributes of culture based on the seminal work of leading scholars in the area: (1) *Shared*: Culture resides in shared behaviors, assumptions, beliefs, and experiences of organizational members. (2) *Persuasive*: Culture permeates different levels and units in the organization and influences from top management decisions to frontline workers' communications and actions. It can be manifested in behaviors, physical environments, organizational policies and rituals, symbols, logos, and stories. (3) *Enduring*: Culture is developed over time and can reinforce itself through the attraction-selection-attrition model (Schneider, 1987). That is, people are attracted to a company if they share similar values and characteristics. Leaders and organizations are also more likely to select those who can fit in. On the contrary, those who cannot fit in tend to leave the company. While culture can change, often through critical events over time, the influence of imprinted values on organizational members can be long-lasting. (4) *Implicit*: Although culture can be manifested in different observable forms (e.g., a behavior or story), it is rooted in collective assumptions and beliefs of people, which is below the surface of the organizational activities. It acts as a "silent language" in an organization that people can sense and respond to.

Types of effective startup culture

While there may not be a standard what a successful startup culture looks like, previous research on organizational culture and entrepreneurship has provided abundant insights. Our research on Chinese startups and entrepreneurs also generated some conclusions with regard to the types of culture that are prevalent or particularly welcomed at startups in China. Although some startups are dominated by one type of culture, others embrace different ones.

Innovation

Innovation is at the core of all startups. Thus, finding that the innovation culture emerged as one of the major themes from our interviews with Chinese entrepreneurs is no surprise. According to our interviewees, innovation culture involves encouragement of risk-taking and trial and error, promoting and rewarding new ideas, approaches, and processes, regardless of who initiated it, being a co-founder or an intern, and recruiting the right people who are curious with an adventurous aptitude. Innovation culture fosters thinking outside of the box and being bold enough to think "wild" or "crazy." "Innovate or die." A startup needs to keep launching new ideas, products, services, or business models. Otherwise, it may soon lose the battleground in the fiercely competitive entrepreneurial environment. A case in illustration is how Hai Di Lao, now a renowned hot pot brand in China, launched its delivery business in its earlier stage based on an idea from one of its employees so that customers can enjoy the experience of hot pot outdoors.

Openness

Gone are the days that you hide information from people, especially in the increasingly transparent era today with the aid of new technologies and the new generation in China who are more informed and better educated (Atherton & Newman, 2017). Stakeholders are demanding more information from organizations. For example, for a startup that sells agricultural products online, consumers are curious about where the products are from, where they were grown, and whether any chemicals were used in the process. A closed-door policy is no longer an option. Instead, an open culture that values transparency, feedback, various voices and perspectives, and adaptability to changes is promoted among entrepreneurs to encourage innovation and build trust and relationships (Men et al., 2018). As Yuan, CEO of a SaaS startup based in Hangzhou, commented:

> We hope to instill a sense of equality and openness in our employees. That's why our management team [members] do not have separate offices. We sit with employees. . . . Freedom and openness are valued in our culture. We respect every voice from every individual.

Inclusiveness and participation

Relatedly, a culture of inclusiveness and participation is advocated by many entrepreneurs in China. Startups with an inclusive and participative culture value inputs from various stakeholders, show willingness to listen, and involve stakeholders in the decision-making process. For instance, an agricultural online retail startup formed an informal think tank. It comprised 50 members of the founders' friends and families whom the CEO met with for regular consultation and feedback. "We listen to whomever is right. The idea does not have to come from the inside," the CEO said.

When stakeholders' ideas and suggestions are taken and implemented by a startup, it conveys a message of respect and inclusiveness. People who come up with the ideas tend to feel empowered, proud, and involved as they see their voices making a difference. Being able to participate essentially gives people a sense of ownership and responsibility. According to Bresciani and Eppler (2010), an important motivator for people to join startups is that their ideas are recognized and they have more opportunities to participate in the decision-making process. As Yuan remarked, "We involve our employees in many things, from naming the company to furnishing the offices. . . . Employees engage mostly when they feel needed, have sufficient freedom and autonomy, and feel trusted."

The culture of inclusiveness and participation and a sense of equality and empowerment perhaps have become more important for Chinese startups than ever before (Atherton & Newman, 2018). The Chinese Panel Study of Entrepreneurial Dynamics reported that the average age of nascent entrepreneurs in China is 31 years old Cumming, Firth, Hou, & Lee (2015). The new generation of entrepreneurs and employees is better educated, more open-minded, and has a more global mindset than their precursors. They hold a set of different values from previous generations, for instance, being more individualistic and autonomous and less deferential to hierarchy and authority (Atherton & Newman, 2018) and valuing equality and originality. As such, they desire being respected and recognized for individual efforts, personalities, and differences. An equal, inclusive, and participative culture, therefore, not only promotes new ideas and innovation at startups but also attracts and retains talents.

Supportiveness and people orientation

A supportive and people-oriented culture is featured by care, sharing, voluntary helping, collaboration, and a genuine concern of employees' well-being. As a traditionally collectivist society, values, such as considering group interests over individual gains, emphasis on collaboration and consultation over competition, stressing harmony and relationships, and sensitivity to human feelings (*renqing*), are still preserved today in China, even though individualistic values are also prevalent among the new generation. Rooted in such relationship-oriented Chinese culture, many startups advocate values of supportiveness, empathy, and compassion when treating employees. For instance, Yao Wang Technology, a social marketing startup based in Hangzhou, offers help to new hires with relocation and house hunting and provides their children with daycare and school arrangements. Hai Di Lao, from its startup stage, has treated employees with care and dignity. As many of its employees are migrant workers from rural areas whose families are in poor living conditions, one of Hai Di Lao's reward policies for their "employees of the month" is to provide their parents a parental subsidy on a monthly basis.

Our research shows that entrepreneurs in China value an atmosphere where employees have close ties, trust one another, and work together as a big family. Although this situation may become challenging when more employees get on board with the growth of a startup, people enjoy the closeness, spontaneous interactions, and deep mutual understanding formed in the early stage. As Yue, CEO of an agricultural online retail startup, noted:

> We don't treat our people as employees; we are brothers and sisters. We have strong bond and sense of collaboration. [That's probably why] when problems arise, they get resolved very quickly. We come to work

every day happily, enjoy communicating with one another, and do meaningful things together.

Competitiveness/aggressiveness

The startup environment is naturally competitive. Twelve thousands startups are born in China every day, 90% of which fail within 18 months (Schuman, 2016). To keep their competitive advantage and survive at the very least, start-ups have to move fast, be tough, and competitive. Most entrepreneurs work under constant pressure. According to Capman (2018), entrepreneurs are 50% more likely to report a mental health condition. As Jian, CEO of a social marketing startup commented, "Being competitive is a must for all startups. Employees and investors are counting on leaders and expecting their return." Qin, CEO of an O2O (online to offline) tailor and wardrobe consulting startup, also noted that at their monthly employee meeting, she analyzes the competitive environment they are facing and discusses where they did well and what can be improved to better handle the competition. A competitive/aggressive culture often comes with high performance. Employees are united by a drive for success and achievement and leaders emphasize goal attainment (Groysberg et al., 2018). The high performance demonstrated by China's tech giant Huawei also benefited from its famous aggressive "wolf" culture developed in its early stage. As Ren Zhengfei, founder and CEO of Huawei, once explained:

> We have a "wolf" spirit in our company. In the battle with lions, wolves have terrifying abilities. With a strong desire to win and no fear of losing, they stick to the goal firmly, making the lions exhausted in every possible way.

In addition, facing fierce competition on a day-to-day basis, many startup leaders are equipped with a sense of urgency and crisis awareness: "Always prepare for the worst" (危机意识). Chinese entrepreneurs generally share the sentiment that the startup and market environment are highly unstable and unpredictable; therefore, they need to stay proactive and be prepared for the worst-case scenario even in the good days. Traditional Chinese idioms, such as "Be prepared for danger in times of peace" (居安思危) and "Amend the window before it rains" (未雨绸缪), contain wisdom on pre-crisis management. This management philosophy has been adopted by many Chinese entrepreneurs. In special times, it can prevent a crisis or even save a company.

Fun and joy

Despite the pressure that entrepreneurs are facing, many of them celebrate a culture of fun and joy. Such culture aims to create a lighthearted work environment. People cherish playfulness, a sense of humor, and excitement in their work. Similarly, in big corporations, a culture of joy and fun at startups can be contagious, creating an enjoyable and happy atmosphere inside out (Men & Robinson, 2018). With a joyful experience at work, employees are more likely to walk the extra mile (Coyle-Shapiro & Shore, 2007). This case is particularly relevant in the highly competitive, fast-paced, and stressful startup environment. Yuan, CEO of a SaaS startup, commented, "We work hard and play hard." Many entrepreneurs we talked to in China shared how they created a culture of fun and joy. For instance, a data service startup based in Hangzhou celebrated its periodical milestone by treating employees with crawfish (a popular street food in China). When they celebrated the company's achievement of two billion users, they ordered 200 pounds of crawfish for their employees. Even customers were invited to the big crawfish feast, which made local media headlines. Other startups organize outing activities for employees, such as karaoke, hiking, chess, or short trips to local attractions. As Yue, CEO of an agricultural online retail startup, commented:

> Our goal is to make everyone enjoy working with us. We eat well and play well. Since our product is about happy living, in the future, we will also build a happy living lab. We will explore what life means and what happy life means, and present and communicate the meaning of happiness in our products to our consumers.

As of today, the startup has moved into a new location. As Yue promised, their establishment is equipped with a gourmet kitchen loaded with many innovative appliances for employees to make fun food experiments.

What shapes startup culture in China?

National culture

To understand startup culture in China, one needs to recognize its external and internal influences at both macro- and micro-levels. He, Lu, and Qian (2019) argued that cultural context plays a fundamental role in shaping value orientations and entrepreneurs' cognitions. Some psychological attributes of entrepreneurs, such as their risk-taking propensity, can be largely affected by the general cultural context in the society. In their book *Entrepreneurship in China*, Atherton and Newman (2018) thoroughly discussed how the historical, political, social, and cultural factors influence entrepreneurship in China today. For instance, the authors argued that in a *masculine* culture, such as that of China, financial and material achievements are valued and prioritized, which is more conducive to entrepreneurial activities. This case may also explain the controversial "996" work schedule (i.e., a work day starts at 9 a.m. and ends at 9 p.m. for six days a week), which is prevalent in the tech industry in China, particularly at startups. In addition, China is considered a *diffuse* culture, in which people find overlap between their personal and work lives and may discuss personal issues at work and business issues at social occasions. Thus, business negotiations and deals in China that are done at a dinner table or a karaoke bar are common. Businesses are also often times discussed via WeChat, a popular instant message and social networking mobile application in China. Such practices are also carried out often by Chinese entrepreneurs.

Under Hofstede's cultural dimensions, the *long-term orientation* in Chinese culture, in which people tend to think long term and value perseverance over short-term and immediate needs, is also reflected in the Chinese startup culture. Such culture may partially explain why many entrepreneurs plan for potential crises in good times and why they take time to develop business relationships with a variety of key stakeholders, such as consumers, suppliers, the media, and government officials. Furthermore, as mentioned earlier, China, as a traditionally collectivist society, has evolved over decades. The new generation in China embraces both *collectivist values*, such as collaboration, relationship, group interests, and harmony, and *individualistic values*, such as competition, uniqueness, and individual differences (Atherton & Newman, 2018). The millennial entrepreneurs are better educated and global-minded, with many having experiences studying or working overseas. They have grown up in an era where Eastern and Western culture have met, with the influence of globalization, internationalization, and technological advancements. Returnee entrepreneurs (i.e., those who studied or worked overseas and come back to China for startups) and foreign investors have also brought in Western business models, management philosophies, cultural values, and practices. In our research, many Chinese entrepreneurs shared that they try to promote a Silicon Valley culture, where they value openness, equality, and free exchange of ideas. As Yuan, a returnee entrepreneur shared, he does not want to be addressed by his title or hold a separate office as the CEO of the company. Instead, he prefers to work in an open space with other employees. Yi, CEO of a big data service startup that offers push notifications for mobile app developers, also noted that he adopted Google's "TGIF" and hosts informal stand-up meetings with employees every Monday, where any topic can be brought up by anyone in the company and discussed openly.

Guanxi, broadly referred to as individuals' social networks and relationships, is a widely known and studied cultural concept in China. Rooted in the Confucian culture, where individuals are considered a part of a community and a set of relationships with family and friends, guanxi is relational and instrumental (Batjargal & Liu, 2004) and is regarded as social capital that provides access to information and resources for organizations (Chen, Chang, & Lee, 2015). For instance, good guanxi with government officials and political leaders helps entrepreneurs obtain information regarding new regulations or policy changes, which may potentially impact their new businesses. Strong ties with news reporters may get the startups' stories out ahead of its competitors. Long-term guanxi with suppliers may get startups a lower purchase price. A study on private equity in China showed the important role that guanxi plays in venture capital practices (Bruton & Ahlstrom, 2003). Regardless of whether special favors are exchanged, guanxi in China can help business run more smoothly. Consequentially, Chinese entrepreneurs tend to spend significant time and efforts developing networks and relationships with customers, investors, suppliers, or other key stakeholders. Good guanxi is also associated with trust, understanding, and loyalty, which reduce risks and costs of doing business (Atherton & Newman, 2018). Research has shown that entrepreneurs have larger social networks than non-entrepreneurs in China (Yueh, 2007), which highlights the importance of relationships to entrepreneurial activity especially in China's collectivist society.

In a nutshell, startup culture in China at the macro level has been influenced by the society's cultural values in China. The social and cultural environment ultimately influences the startup players – the entrepreneurs' and their key stakeholders' cognitions and beliefs (He, Lu, & Qian, 2019). In the meantime, one needs to recognize the impact of external forces (e.g., culture, technology, and investment) beyond the national boarder. After all, in an increasingly globalized and connected business environment, no company can operate in isolation. These mega factors provide an important context for understanding the specifics of startup culture in China.

Startup founders/leaders

At the micro level, the argument that startup founders and leaders shape startup culture seems to be a general consensus. Some argue startup culture starts to form as soon as the company is created. Startup founders and their characters, beliefs, and values thus serve as the DNA of a startup culture (Men et al., 2018). At the very early stage, the founding team, often comprising startup leaders, envisions where the startup is headed to, defines the core values and principles that guide the company's decision-making and actions, and recruits talent that "fits" its culture. Research has identified four qualities of startup leaders that contribute to entrepreneurial success: (1) opportunism, which refers to being informed, alert, and attuned to future trends and new business opportunities; (2) proactivity, which is the tendency to be proactive in getting things accomplished (this quality is also related to energy, confidence, and self-determination); (3) creativity, which means non-conformity, originality, preference for novel experiences, and a tendency to generate innovative business ideas; and (4) vision, which features the ability to see a bigger picture, have a higher sense of purpose, and to create culture and drive change (Akhtar & Ort, 2018).

Research has suggested that background, personality, management philosophies, and communication styles of founders/leaders can all have an impact on startup culture. For instance, a startup CEO's detail orientation and perfectionism tend to be reflected in the high-quality products/services the company offers. A caring, responsive, empathetic, and friendly startup leader may contribute to a people-oriented culture of the startup (Men et al., 2018). By contrast, a founder with a military background and assertive management style can cultivate an aggressive and ruthless company culture, such as Huawei's "wolf" culture. Another typical example is how Tony Hsieh's personality and management communication style shaped Zappos' "fun and a little weird" culture in the earlier years (Askin, Petriglieri, & Lockard, 2016). As the CEO of the company, Hsieh kept things casual, wearing jeans, sneakers, or a hoodie each day. He communicated in a casual matter, writing emails ignoring capital letters and punctuation and using bullet points. He also preferred to greet others using a hug instead of a formal handshake. Tony was also among the first CEOs to embrace social media communication. He developed a large following on Twitter as he believed social media can make people happier because of its transparency nature and allowed him to develop closer connections and bonding with Zappos' customers and employees.

As noted by Swiercz and Lydon (2002), creating and influencing startup culture is one of the core competencies for startup leaders. At startups, leaders define what the culture looks like and communicate about it. Essentially, it is the startup leaders' job to communicate with key stakeholders on who they are, what they believe in, what they intend to accomplish, and how they can get there (Ruvio, Rosenblatt, & Hertz-Lazarowitz, 2010). In this sense, startup leaders are the company's storytellers; their communications, verbally and nonverbally, online and offline, can influence how the startup is perceived by various stakeholders. Furthermore, in the startup context, leaders interact with employees on a daily basis; startup founders and leaders are considered role models, sometimes even idols of employees. Employees look up to startup leaders for behavior standards, and leaders thus need to symbolize and bring into life the values they advocate (Akhtar & Ort, 2018). In sum, startup leaders shape organizational culture through conscious and unconscious actions over time.

Building a successful startup culture

Now the question comes, how can startups develop a successful culture, a culture that actually works? Apparently, no one-size-for-all approach is available, but some insights drawn from previous research and our research data may provide a basic roadmap for entrepreneurs.

1 *Identify the distinctiveness.* A startup starts with an innovative idea and serves a unique purpose. Before defining the cultural values, startup leaders should carefully analyze themselves and their firms. Such analysis should include their products/services, operations, goals and objectives, characteristics of the founding members, and the internal and external environments. Founders need to be clear about what the startup's core is, what makes the startup unique and competitive, why it exists, and what the company intends to achieve in the future. This prerequisite is often associated with conversations around the company's vision, which is fundamentally a compass that guides the organization's decisions and activities and a powerful means through which leaders communicate organization goals to employees (Ruvio et al., 2010). Once a vision/mission has been established, ideally based on collective efforts of early members of the startup, leaders can gradually determine the values that match the vision, align them with the goals, and reflect the characters of the startup members.

2 *Define culture values.* As mentioned earlier, culture is shared values, beliefs, and assumptions among organizational members that guide their behaviors. A healthy and effective culture creates a benign work environment that keeps employees and attracts talent that fits. Thus, clearly defining what culture values (e.g., customer/employee first, integrity, excellence, equality, and empowerment) they want to stand by and advocate for and how they are aligned with Chinese societal culture is critical for startup leaders. As culture is collectively developed over time, identifying what a startup wants its culture to be like from the beginning, be it people oriented, aggressive, or open and fun, is necessary.

3 *Articulate the culture.* Once the underlying values and beliefs are defined, they need to be communicated and articulated to the internal and external stakeholders. Stories need to be told; continuous conversations and discussions among founding members and employees are essential to interpret and reinforce the culture. Culture communication apparently starts from the top – startup leaders need to convey what the values are, how they define who they are, and how they should be implemented in their daily operations, research and development, sales, customer services, and strategic communication. For instance, to live by Zappos' cultural value of "delivering WOW through service," Tony Hsieh emphasized

developing personal connections with customers. He directed customer representatives to be authentic on the phone and develop a "genuine relationship" with each customer (Askin et al., 2016).

4   *Recruit people who fit and align.* Startup competitions come down to the competition of talents. In our research, a common sentiment shared among the entrepreneurs was the difficulty of recruiting the right people. Limited in human resources, knowledge, and time, startups often hire based on needed skill sets. However, one important aspect that should be considered by startup leaders is hiring based on culture fit. It is also instrumental in establishing the startup culture. Does the person share the values you believe in? Are they motivated by the vision that you portray for the company and personally connected to the purpose of the business? Take Zappos again, for example. The company's interview regarding "culture fit" weighs 50% in its hiring. A candidate will not be invited to meet the hiring manager or other employees of Zappos until they pass the cultural fit interview.

5   *Training and reward system.* Reinforcement of culture is as important if not more than building a culture. New employee training is an opportunity to imprint the startup's cultural values on new comers. As culture is represented in how things are said and done in an organization, training should go beyond simple knowledge and skills and include incorporating culture and values. In addition, a reward system should be in place to reinforce behaviors that promote or symbolize the startup culture. The reward can be monetary incentive or informal recognitions and acknowledgements. For instance, some startups feature an "employee of the month" in their newsletters or on social media who demonstrate certain aspects of the startup culture. In this way, not only do the recognized individuals feel encouraged, but others will also be motivated to follow these behaviors.

6   *Role modeling.* To make culture come into life, startups need to provide concrete examples, tell vivid stories, and feature role models. Startups can always identify top-performing employees who showcase the organizational culture, and the "role model" function of startup leaders/CEOs cannot be underestimated. Culture is led and communicated from the top. Leaders should walk the talk and make sure that their communications and actions stay true to cultural values of the startup. In this sense, leaders as role models for employees bear no difference from those in big corporations, except that startup leaders tend to interact with employees more closely and frequently, amplifying their role model effects.

7   *Measuring culture success.* Lastly, culture building efforts need to be assessed. Are cultural values of the startup well received and understood among employees and other stakeholders? Is the startup culture aligned with startup goals and objectives? Is it making an impact on

startup employees' motivation, satisfaction, and engagement in the organization? How is the startup culture tied to the growth of the business? To assess culture effectiveness, startups should implement measures to collect feedback, frequently and thoroughly, from employees. Given the small size of startups, informal methods, such as observations and one-on-one and group conversations, can be carried out to listen to employees. For those who utilize social media, such as Sina Weibo or WeChat, to engage with consumers, social listening assisted with built-in analytical tools can provide cost-effective data from external publics. When needed, formal surveys can provide numeric and generalizable information for startups to assess its cultural consequences.

In sum, startup culture, as shared values, beliefs, assumptions, and experiences in the entrepreneurial context, is shaped and lived by its members. Startup culture in China, although rooted in Chinese societal culture today, which is collective and individualistic, relationship oriented, diffused, and long-term focused, is ultimately created by startup founders. The character, personality, management philosophy, and communication styles of these founders imprint on the values of the startup. In this chapter, we enlist six types of startup culture that have been discussed as effective by entrepreneurs we interviewed. Ultimately, what works best is what works for *your* startup. Culture, despite taking time and efforts to build, is a primary lever for organizations, including startups, to maintain organizational viability and effectiveness. Startup leaders should be aware of cultural implications and take proactive actions, whenever possible, to cultivate a positive startup culture that is consequential for entrepreneurial success.

References

Akhtar, R., & Ort, O. (2018, April). Building entrepreneurial teams: Talent, social capital, and culture. *People & Strategy*. Retrieved from www.rhrinternational. com/sites/default/files/content/Building%20Entrepreneurial%20Teams%20-%20 Talent%2C%20Social%20Capital%2C%20and%20Culture.pdf

Askin, N., Petriglieri, G., & Lockard, J. (2016). Tony Hsieh at Zappos: Structure, culture, and change. *INSEAD*, IN1249.

Atherton, A. M., & Newman, A. (2017). *Entrepreneurship in China: The emergence of the private sector*. London: Routledge.

Batjargal, B., & Liu, M. M. (2004). Entrepreneurs' access to private equity in China: The role of social capital. *Organization Science*, *15*(2), 159–172.

Bresciani, S., & Eppler, M. (2010). Brand new ventures? Insights on startups' branding practices. *Journal of Product & Brand Management*, *19*, 356–366. doi:10.1108/ 10610421011068595

Bruton, G. D., & Ahlstrom, D. (2003). An institutional view of China's venture capital industry: Explaining the differences between China and the West. *Journal of Business Venturing*, *18*(2), 233–259.

Chapman, J. (2018). Investors and entrepreneurs need to address the mental health crisis in startups. *Techcrunch*. Retrieved from https://techcrunch.com/2018/12/30/investors-and-entrepreneurs-need-to-address-the-mental-health-crisis-in-startup-culture/

Chen, M.-H., Chang, Y.-Y., & Lee, C.-Y. (2015). Creative entrepreneurs' guanxi networks and success: Information and resource. *Journal of Business Research*, *68*, 900–905.

Coyle-Shapiro, J. A.-M., & Shore, L. M. (2007). The employee – organization relationship: Where do we go from here? *Human Resource Management Review*, *17*(2), 166–179. doi.org/10.1016/j.hrmr.2007.03.008

Cumming, D, Firth, M., Hou, W., & Lee, E. (2015). *Developments in Chinese entrepreneurship: Key issues and challenges*. UK: Palgrave MacMillan.

Groysberg, B., Lee, J., Price, J., & Cheng, J. Y-J. (2018, January-February). The leader's guide to corporate culture: Changing your organization's culture can improve its performance. Here's how to do that. *Harvard Business Review*. Retrieved from https://www.spencerstuart.com/~/media/pdf%20files/research%20and%20insight%20pdfs/the-leaders-guide-to-corporate-culture.pdf

He, C., Lu, J., & Qian, H. (2019). Entrepreneurship in China. *Small Business Economics*, *52*, 563–572.

Men, L. R., Ji, Y. G., & Chen, Z. F. (2017). Dialogues with entrepreneurs in China: How startup companies cultivate relationships with strategic publics. *Journal of Public Relations Research*, *29*(2–3), 90–113. DOI: 10.1080/1062726X.2017.1329736

Men, L. R., & Robinson, K. (2018). It's about how the employees feel! Examining the impact of emotional culture on employee-organization relationships. *Corporate Communications: An International Journal*. 10.1108/CCIJ-05-2018-0065

Rauch, A., Wiklund, J., Lumpkin, G. T., & Frese, M. (2009). Entrepreneurial orientation and business performance: An assessment of past research and suggestions for the future. *Entrepreneurship Theory and Practice*, *33*(3), 761–787.

Ruvio, A., Rosenblatt, Z., & Hertz-Lazarowitz, R. (2010). Entrepreneurial leadership vision in nonprofit vs. for-profit organizations. *The Leadership Quarterly*, *21*, 144–158.

Schneider, B. (1987). The people make the place. *Personnel Psychology*, *40*, 437–453.

Schuman, M. (2016, September 3). Venture communism: How China is building a startup boom. *The New York Times*.

Sriramesh, K., Grunig, J. E., & Buffington, J. (1992). Corporate culture and public relations. In J. E. Grunig (Ed.), *Excellence in public relations and communication management* (pp. 577–598). Hillsdale, NJ: Lawrence Erlbaum Associates.

Swiercz, P. M., & Lydon, S. R. (2002). Entrepreneurial leadership in high-tech firms: A field study. *Leadership & Organization Development Journal*, *23*(7), 380–389.

Yueh, L. (2007). China's entrepreneurs. Discussion Paper, Department of Economics, University of Oxford, Oxford.

7 Entrepreneurial leadership communication

A startup fails for many known reasons, but a critical factor that determines the long-term success of a new venture is entrepreneurial leadership (Swiercz & Lydon, 2002). By definition, entrepreneurial leadership entails "influencing and directing the performance of group members toward the achievement of organizational goals that involve recognizing and exploiting entrepreneurial opportunities" (Renko, Tarabishy, Carsrud, & Brännback, 2015, p. 55). As entrepreneurial leadership can exist in organizations of any type, size, or development stage, it is particularly relevant and essential for startups. Furthermore, founders must lead, create, and innovate, as no standard operating procedures, management practices, or organizational structures that serve as bases for new ventures are currently available (Hmieleski & Ensley, 2007).

In the startup context, entrepreneurial leaders generally refer to founding CEOs who established the venture and make key strategic decisions for the organization (Kang, Solomon, & Choi, 2015). They are the most influential persons in startups and are in charge of critical tasks, such as creating visions and goals, identifying and developing new business opportunities, attracting investors, recruiting, and inspiring and motivating employees toward the creation and implementation of new ideas and creative solutions (Kuratko, 2007). Without a doubt, entrepreneurial leadership forms a central competitive advantage of startups and is essential to the growth and sustainability of the new venture.

Leadership can hardly be implemented without effective communication (J. Mayfield & M. Mayfield, 2017). Communication constructs leadership and intertwines with many aspects of leadership practices. Robinson's definition of leadership argues that "leadership is exercised when thoughts expressed in talk or action are recognized by others as capable of progressing tasks or problems which are important to them" (Robinson, 2001, p. 93). It also pinpoints the connection between leadership and communication. In this chapter, we review important issues related to founding CEOs' leadership communication in startups, especially in the context of China, including communication purposes, strategies, and channels.

Purposes of entrepreneurial leadership communication

Given the unique stage, needs, and characteristics of startups, entrepreneurial leadership communication for new ventures serves several key purposes internally and externally, including articulating the vision, defining/constructing culture values, advocating for the brand, managing investor relations, recruiting and managing talents, and building trust.

Vision communication

Vision is central to entrepreneurial process and affects entrepreneurs' actions and long-term journey in building the new venture (Ruvio, Rosenblatt, & Hertz-Lazarowitz, 2010). As part of a business strategy, a clear vision sets the goals of the startup and inspires people to strive toward a greater purpose. This role is particularly critical for startups when the corporate identity is yet to be built. Vision tells the world the purpose of the new venture; its importance in a broader social, cultural, and economic context; and its future projection. Successful visions can help startup leaders attract, unite, and motivate employees, instill confidence in its investors and customers, and drive the team toward the same goal. The CEO of a community transportation and ride-sharing startup in China elaborated the importance of vision communication in our interview: "We need to convince the public that what we are doing is something meaningful and great. Our business is not only about making money; we are creating value for the society." In addition, our quantitative survey of 1,027 employees who work for various startups in China showed that startup leaders' vision communication is strongly correlated with perceived leadership credibility (Pearson correlation $r = .44$), employee identification with the startup ($r = .43$), their level of trust in the startup ($r = .47$), and intention to stay ($r = .52$).

The startup founder's job is to create, communicate about, and live the vision of the organization. When China's Internet giant Alibaba Group launched an IPO in 2014, a video clip of its founder and former chairman, Jack Ma, went viral. In the video, Jack Ma was speaking to his co-founders and first set of employees when the company was founded in 1999 about the vision of the company. In his talk, he addressed the question, "What will Alibaba become in future?" In retrospect, what the company has been striving for in the past decade "to make it easy to do business anywhere" has guided its strategies and operations, leading its development as today's global e-commerce empire. As Jack Ma noted in his famous remark, "We need to have a dream; what if the dream becomes true?" For a startup, its dream is its vision. Without communicating the vision repeatedly, clearly, and compellingly by the leader, it cannot be seen or implemented.

Defining/constructing culture values

Culture values represent the belief system of an organization. Swiercz and Lydon (2002) discussed creating and influencing startup culture as one of the core functional competencies for entrepreneurial leaders. According to these authors, the development and preservation of culture is a "conscious decision" made by startup founders (p. 9). More than often, startup leaders gather inputs from the top management team to identify the core ideologies, principles, and values of the business, which forms the foundation of the company's identity and culture. Just as vision can unite and motivate employees, culture can attract talents who share similar values, determine how things get done in the firm, and even become part of the startup's brand and image.

Our research on entrepreneurs and startups in China has confirmed the impact of startup leaders' character, personality traits, and communication on the climate and culture of the organization. Startup founders are not only the DNA of the startup; they are also the living symbols who bring the cultural values into light and implement them in action. Startup leaders are considered role models by their employees. Given the small-sized and relatively intimate environment, startup employees can easily observe and model leaders' behaviors and directly interact with them (Men, Chen, & Ji, 2018). Unlike in large corporations, where CEOs are usually seen from afar or on the screen, startup leaders are real, personal, and visually present, making their influence immediate and local. Thus leaders need to define, live by, and communicate about the culture values to build an effective startup culture. Jian, the CEO of a social marketing startup, commented, "We need to walk the talk and show everyone what kind of culture we want to build."

Brand advocacy and management

As startups usually lack an established public relations department in the early stages, startup leaders, such as founders and CEOs, often act as informal public relations agents who advocate for their brand. Thus, it is not uncommon to see that startup CEOs speak at industry events, show up on entrepreneurial reality shows, such as "Win in China" (赢在中国) and "Entrepreneurs in China" (创客中国), write blogs, post on behalf of the company on WeChat, Sina Weibo, or TikTok; or even write handwritten notes to their top customers. Cohen (2015) identified brand management as one of the six most important roles of startup CEOs, along with cash flow, vision, team building, investor management, and corporate development. Rus, Ruzzier, and Ruzzier (2018) described the roles of startup founders and CEOs in startup branding. In their model, named "startup branding funnel," entrepreneurs need to investigate the industry, competitors, customers, and resources available in the company in the initial stage of startup branding. Simply, the leaders need to be aware of what others are doing in the industry to decide how to develop and strengthen their own brand. Then, in the development phase of branding, startup leaders need to engage in storytelling and develop narratives and anecdotes to convey the attributes, benefits, values, personality, and relationships related to the brand. In other words, the unique features of the brand, the benefits of the brand for the consumers, the cultural beliefs of the startup, and the influence of such cultural briefs on the community should be identified

Managing investor relations

For venture-backed startups, investors are among the most important key stakeholders as they provide financial support and other helpful resources. A serial entrepreneur, Zhan, who is currently the CEO of an e-commerce startup in Hangzhou, noted in our interview, "Besides providing money, our investors also assist us in recruiting top talent in the field to fill in core positions, maintaining key client relationships, and developing new business endeavors." The role of the startup CEO or founder is to manage investor relations. Getting investors to invest in the startup is their job in the first place. Then, they need to keep the investors in the loop and maintain relationships with them. As Cohen (2015) remarked, "Keeping . . . investors informed, helpful and happy is one of the most underrated things that CEOs can do to improve their chances of success." In our research of Chinese entrepreneurs, a similar notion was observed by Hang, the co-founder and CEO of a 3D home design startup. Hang commented, "You have to communicate with investors proactively and periodically to keep them updated and informed." Good relationships with investors, which are managed by startup CEOs, help with subsequent rounds of venture funding and bring in new resources.

Recruiting and managing talents (team building)

People are the core and drivers of the success of a new venture. As startups often do not have sufficient resources for recruiting or training programs or an established human resources system, many startup leaders choose to take charge of recruiting themselves. A question that the CEOs have to constantly think about is whether the right people are in the right place. After all, "Without the right captains leading the ships, there's little chance they'll continue traveling in the right direction" (Cohen, 2015). Thus, startup leaders need to be in a "selling" mode 100% of their time, talking about the company at every opportunity, at lunches, networking events, and socials, to attract new talents. They also need to make tough decisions and communicate when they have to let go of the bad apples who are negatively affecting the performance of the team. As our data show, team building is among the top communication priorities of startup leaders.

Building credibility, confidence, and trust

Startups in the early stages face many challenges, including lack of established brand and credibility. Startups usually face doubts and scrutiny from customers, investors, media, and employees on whether they can deliver what they promise, their prospects, or why they should believe in the startups. Thus, building credibility of the brand and establishing confidence and trust among key stakeholders are two of the key purposes of startup leadership communication. With recognition of the powerful effect of CEO personal branding in establishing startup credibility, many entrepreneurs in China opt for actively building and managing their personal image by participating in industry events, giving public speeches, and competing for entrepreneurial individual awards sponsored by various organizations at regional and national levels, such as "Entrepreneurial Heroes" and "Top 10 Entrepreneur Award." Countless startup CEOs in China are also widely recognized celebrities or thought leaders, such as Yonghao Luo of Smartisan Co., Ltd., Xing Meng of Helijia, Inc., and Danyang Li of Nicomama, Inc. While it is important to build credibility among external stakeholders, such as consumers, customers, and investors, it is paramount in instilling confidence in employees and building trust internally because employees are the driving force for innovation and development in startups and are also the most trustworthy ambassadors and brand advocates.

Strategies of entrepreneurial leadership communication

Now that we have discussed why startup leaders need to communicate, we turn to the question of "How?" How can startup founders and CEOs effectively communicate to build brand, manage relationships internally and externally, and establish credibility, confidence, and trust among stakeholders? The entrepreneurial leadership communication strategies are presented as follows.

Portraying a compelling vision

Vision communication is a critical component of startup brand building (Rus et al., 2018). Although the definition of vision varies, it generally refers to an idealized goal to be achieved in the future. A good and compelling vision needs to be future oriented, "optimistic, desirably, challenging, clear, brief, and achievable" (Ruvio et al., 2010, p. 145). In the startup context, a vision is the company's compass and is often the result of the entrepreneur's intuitive and holistic thinking about the startup, which bridges its current situation and future state. It reflects the shared values to which the startup and everyone in it should aspire. In motivating language theory, Jacqueline Mayfield and Milton Mayfield (2018) noted that vision should be inspirational and transcend the financial and performance goals of the organization. Therefore, for vision communication, startup leaders need to invoke a collective, higher purpose among stakeholders and connect with them at a personal level. Startup employees should be able to find meaning in their job and see how their work contributes value to the big picture and higher purpose of the new venture. The entrepreneurial vision statement should also reflect the new venture's uniqueness, such as the type of venture (e.g., for-profit vs. non-profit), organizational context, and entrepreneurs' goals and aspirations for the business (Ruvio et al., 2010).

Embracing transparency

Communication and public relations scholars in Western society have consistently demonstrated the positive effects of transparent communication on employee outcomes, such as trust, employee-organization relationships, identification with the organization, and employee engagement (Jiang & Men, 2015; Rawlins, 2009). Likewise, our recent quantitative data from a survey of 1,027 startup employees in China reveal strong positive associations among startup leaders' transparent communication, featured by providing substantial, unbiased, and accountable information in a timely manner based on employees' information needs, perceived trustworthiness ($r = .57$) and authenticity ($r = .80$) of the entrepreneur, employee trust of the startup ($r = .65$), and level of employee engagement ($r = .66$). In other words, the more transparent startup leaders communicate, the more they are perceived as trustworthy and authentic, and the more employees tend to trust the startup and engage in their work.

However, despite these data-based benefits of transparent communication, our interview data indicate that radical transparency is not commonly practiced by startup leaders in China. Many of them advocate the idea of "being strategically transparent," which means sharing the right information with the right people at the right time. Although this philosophy is not problematic in practice, it poses an ethical dilemma for startup leaders: who determines what the right information is, who the right people are, and when the right time is. In other words, transparency for whom, the startup or its stakeholders? As Rawlins (2009) noted, transparency is not defined by what the company or leaders want to tell but what the stakeholders want to know. To avoid pseudo-transparency, startup leaders in China need to involve stakeholders to decide information sufficiency and completeness.

Transparent leadership communication is not only about sharing information stakeholders want to know, but it also involves fostering an open environment, proactively keeping stakeholders in the loop, and providing clear task and role expectations and directions, all of which are essential for startups. In the unstable entrepreneurial environment with high uncertainties, startup leaders being open, transparent, up-front, and approachable can help reduce uncertainly, relieve anxiety, and build trust among employees. It also helps maintain investor relationships through proactive reporting and updating. As Yuan, founder of a SaaS startup, explained, keeping investors in the loop not only shows respect for them and keeps all parties on the same page but also brings in resources and support in a timely manner. Moreover, transparency in the sense of providing clear expectations and guidelines, referred to as direction-giving language in the motivating language theory, reduces role ambiguity and enhances task clarity, which in turn can lead to reduced turnover and enhanced productivity in the startup (J. Mayfield & M. Mayfield, 2017).

Listening with care and respect

Effective listening is one of the key differentiators of competent leaders and communicators. However, not every leader listens well, as they often focus on what they have to say or what needs to be told. As many communication scholars noted, communication in its recommended two-way form must involve speaking and listening. Listening is essential to achieving mutual understanding, finding the common ground, and initiating a dialogue (Lloyd, Boer, Keller, & Voelpel, 2015; Macnamara, 2016). Research suggests that listening is an important behavior that signals management openness, creates a safe environment for employees to speak up, fosters intimacy, and elicits positive perceptions of the leader (Lloyd et al., 2015). For startups, leaders naturally carry the role of a listener to generate positive perceptions and, more importantly, to constantly gather feedback from various stakeholders and evaluate where they are and how they are doing in a highly turbulent entrepreneurial environment with limited information, high uncertainty, and fast changes.

Listening needs to be practiced in a way that shows care, respect, empathy, acceptance, and a non-judgmental attitude (Lloyd et al., 2015). Such effective leader internal listening has been shown to connect with employees' psychological well-being and personal development (Reis, Sheldon, Gable, Roscoe, & Ryan, 2000). Our survey data also demonstrate that startup leaders' listening behavior in China is linked to perceived leadership responsiveness ($r = .60$) and authenticity ($r = .61$), which is also strongly correlated with employee trust in the startup ($r = .55$) and feeling of shared control and empowerment ($r = .72$).

Startup leaders should also listen to other stakeholders, including customers, investors, partners, and competitors – whoever can provide constructive feedback and information. In our study, many startup CEOs noted the importance of effective listening, and some shared they formed informal advisory groups, which comprise representatives of various stakeholders who periodically meet with the CEO to provide feedback and suggestions. To genuinely listen and demonstrate care and respect, startup leaders need to incorporate stakeholders' voice in the decision-making process. Listening is not a superficial form of simply gathering information. It is more about how the information is used thereafter. In the early stage of startups, CEOs or founders play an important role as the listening agent. Such practice can be systemized with the growth of the startup and conducted at the organizational level. To encourage organizational listening, startup CEOs need to be open-minded; recognize the value of listening; allocate resources, staff, and support with listening technologies; and, more importantly, develop a culture of listening (Macnamara, 2016).

Communicating authenticity and empathy

Authenticity has been recognized as one of the key attributes that characterize effective leadership communication (Men & Bowen, 2017). Authenticity generally refers to being true to one's personality, traits, character, or core values. Synonyms of being authentic include being real, truthful, genuine, consistent, and sincere, as opposed to being dishonest, concealing, distorting, withholding, artificial, and manipulative (Men & Tsai, 2017). Authentic leaders are those who are deeply aware of their values, beliefs, and strengths and weakness and stay true to who they are. They do not behave in accordance with others' expectations but to what they believe is right and their internalized values, such as honesty, fairness, kindness, and accountability. Authentic leaders are open, transparent, and genuine in their communication with others and show consistency in what they say and do (Walumbwa, Avolio, Gardner, Wernsing, & Peterson, 2008).

Startup leaders in China generally recognize the value of authenticity in their communication. As Qin, CEO of an O2O (online to offline) tailor and wardrobe consulting startup, remarked, "Through the years, I've found the easiest and best means to communicate and work with other people is to be yourself, be authentic, and speak the truth." Jian, CEO of a social media marketing and mobile game operation startup, also said, "You have to be authentic and consistent. If you don't deliver what you promised as the leader, employees won't do either." Many startup leaders also recognize the value of being genuine and real, presenting a true self in front of stakeholders. For employees, unlike those in big corporations, startup leaders are approachable, can be seen, and are easy to talk to. The intimate and compact environment affords startup leaders day-to-day opportunities to show who they are, what they believe in, their personality, and the human side of the leadership.

Being personal, authentic, and genuine requires startup leaders to be able to walk in others' shoes and emotionally connect with others. This practice is referred to as leaders' use of empathetic language in Mayfield and Mayfield's motivating language theory. According to the theory, leaders' use of empathetic language, such as praising followers' successful efforts or task accomplishments; conveying messages of care, compassion, and empathy on employees' personal life events; and showing encouragement and support when others encounter challenges, can lead to employee satisfaction, engagement, and positive organizational behavior. Our survey data confirm these theoretical propositions in the entrepreneurial context in China. As new ventures often face challenges, uncertainties, and setbacks given the lack of experience and resources, startup leaders' being able to see others' perspective, empathize, and connect emotionally is undoubtedly an important quality for their leadership communication.

Fostering equality, dialogue, empowerment, and inclusion

People are startups' most important asset (Cohen, 2015). Startups attract talents in a unique way in that it can provide more opportunities for employees to be involved, participate in decision-making, and make a difference. As equality, autonomy, empowerment, and inclusion are often expected at startups, startup leaders need to infuse their communication with these values. Considering that the societal culture in China has transformed from predominantly collectivist to one that recognizes individualism, uniqueness, competitiveness, cooperation, and collectivity (Men & Tsai, 2012), startup leader communication to foster equality and reduce power distance can be appealing to stakeholders today. As many startup CEOs noted in our interviews, they do not want to have separate offices from other employees or be addressed by their titles or last names. They advocate the idea of equality in their communication, where everyone in the startup is appreciated and valued, regardless of their title or position. Furthermore, with limited resources and support, many startup leaders recognize the value of being inclusive in their communication and create dialogue with various stakeholders who can contribute to the organization's strategy formulation. Incorporating customers' feedback and investors' contributions in strategic decision-making empowers these stakeholders and shows respect that nurtures long-term relationships. Internally, giving employees enough autonomy when their interests and competencies are aligned with the job and communicating the idea that employees are trusted can go a long way. As Yuan, CEO of a SaaS startup, remarked, "Don't constrain the employees; give them autonomy and freedom. Let them innovate and do things in their own way. They will go beyond your expectation and surprise you."

Channels of entrepreneurial leadership communication

Startup leaders in China use a variety of channels in their communication with various stakeholders, among which the most frequently used and effective ones were found to be face-to-face communication, mobile messengers, and phones (Men, Chen, & Ji, 2018). Thus, tactics and channels that are commonly used by big corporations, such as internal publications (e.g., newsletters, magazines), emails, corporate TV, on-demand videos/audios, and teleconferencing, are unsurprisingly not prevalent in the startup setting. This finding may be attributed to the particular needs of entrepreneurial communication and the less dispersed and relatively close communication environment at startups.

Face-to-face communication

Face-to-face communication has been consistently argued as one of the most effective and "rich" leadership communication channels given its capability to communicate complex and emotion-loaded information, allowance of immediate feedback and clarification, and availability of non-verbal cues (Daft & Lengel, 1986). Likewise, our research shows that startup leaders in China generally prefer face-to-face venues such as one-on-one meetings in communicating with various stakeholders. On the one hand, the fast-changing, unstable, and highly uncertain startup environment requires startup leaders to communicate complex information to stakeholders in an accurate and efficient manner. They need to ensure that their messages are successfully delivered, clearly heard, and interpreted in the intended way. Face-to-face communication gives the audience the opportunity to ask questions and simultaneously clarify doubts. Startup leaders can also observe how their messages are received through reading non-verbal cues (e.g., a frowning face, a confused/happy look) from the audience. On the other hand, face-to-face communication, either formal or informal, such as one-on-one meetings, group meetings, and informal gatherings, provides startup leaders an important channel to listen, solicit input, and gather feedbacks from stakeholders. The personal touch and authentic element enable people to openly share, allowing stakeholders to voice their opinions and concerns and have a say in the startup's decision-making process.

Informal business functions, such as lunches, dinner, coffee/tea chats, and karaoke outings, are common practices in China. Startup leaders often meet with investors, partners, journalists, or employees over these informal gatherings to discuss businesses or simply to form/deepen relationships. Such practices are partially rooted in the traditional Chinese culture of collectivism and relationship orientation (guanxi), where strong social ties, connections, and networks are valued and impact business success (Men et al., 2018; Luo, Huang, & Wang, 2011). According to a study by Chen, Chang, and Lee (2015), who surveyed 293 entrepreneurs in China, guanxi network influences entrepreneurial success through the mediating factors of information accessibility and resource availability. In particular, family, business (e.g., with distributors, suppliers, competitors, and customers), and community ties (e.g., with industrial associations, labor unions) improve information accessibility. Family and government ties (e.g., with political leaders, government officials) enhance resource availability (Chen et al., 2015).

Mobile messengers

Our interview and survey data both show that mobile messengers, especially WeChat, are most commonly used by startup leaders in communicating with stakeholders. This situation is partially attributed to WeChat's high penetration (93% in tier 1 cities) in the business community in China (Hollander, 2018). Moreover, the convenience, efficiency, and mobility that social messengers afford along with the unique features of WeChat, such as group chat, dual text and audio messages, and social networking ("moments"), make it an unparalleled tool for startup leaders to communicate with various stakeholders in an informal, causal manner. Many startup leaders "befriend" their investors, partners, or journalists on WeChat to stay in touch, facilitate communication, and share company- or product/service-related information to them on "Moments," serving their startups' branding purpose. WeChat groups are commonly used by startup leaders to communicate with team members on non-urgent issues. It mimics a face-to-face group setting due to its multimedia, personal, communal, and relational features.

Startup leaders can easily listen to, observe, and participate in the discussions of different functional WeChat groups built around projects or departments. They can also engage in fun conversations, one-on-one or in groups, with the aid of numerous emojis and stickers available on WeChat to communicate their personalities and characters and build the startup culture.

Phones

Startup leaders in China also use phones to communicate relatively urgent issues with various stakeholders. Although not as commonly used as face-to-face meetings and mobile messengers, when face-to-face option is not available, phone calls can be a preferable channel due to the personal touch, synchronous nature, and rich verbal cues that the device carries (Xia & Mao, 2016). Phones can be efficiently used in coordinating everyday activities, seeking for clarifications, or discussing complex issues. The expressive functions that phone calls have and the availability of human voice also make phones advantageous in communicating emotional support, strengthening connections, and enhancing relationship closeness.

Emails

Unlike in big corporations, email is not commonly used at startups in China but are still referred to by startup leaders as an effective channel for *formal* communication, such as announcing new decisions, major changes, exchanging documents, or submitting work reports. The advantages of an email lie in its ability to reach a widespread audience in a simultaneous and efficient way and its reviewability and revisability (Men & Bowen, 2017). However, this type of communication falls short in its capability to communicate complex or emotion-loaded information due to its lean features.

In sum, entrepreneurial leadership communication serves various purposes that pertain to startups' survival and development, including vision development, culture and identity construction, brand management, investor relations, team building, and establishing confidence and trust among stakeholders. To achieve these goals, startup leaders in China should proactively communicate a compelling vision that is future oriented, purpose driven, challenging, motivating, inspiring, and infused with passion. They should listen with care and respect and have a genuine interest in stakeholders' needs; embrace openness and transparency; be authentic, genuine, consistent, and empathetic; and foster equality, empowerment, inclusion, and real dialogue in their communication. To effectively communicate, startup leaders in China can rely on multiple platforms based on their communication needs and thorough understanding of the features of each channel, for instance, by using face-to-face communication to manage/deepen relationships, mobile messengers for informal and casual conversations, email for formal announcements, and phone calls for communicating urgent matters. The communication competence and skills vary among startup leaders. Fortunately, communication skills can be learned and trained, and capability can be enhanced. To this end, startup leaders need to recognize the importance of entrepreneurial communication and their own role as an informal public relations agent in the new venture context.

References

Chen, M.-H., Chang, Y.-Y., & Lee, C.-Y. (2015). Creative entrepreneurs' guanxi networks and success: Information and resource. *Journal of Business Research*, *68*, 900–905.

Cohen, A. (2015, April 14). The 6 most important roles of a startup CEO. *Entrepreneur*. Retrieved from www.entrepreneur.com/article/244391

Daft, R. L., & Lengel, R. H. (1986). Organizational information requirements: Media richness and structural design. *Management Science*, *32*, 554–571.

Hmieleski, K. M., & Ensley, M. D. (2007). A contextual examination of new venture performance: Entrepreneur leadership behavior, top management team heterogeneity, and environmental dynamism. *Journal of Organizational Behavior*, *28*(7), 865–889.

Hollander, R. (2018, May 6). WeChat has hit 1 billion monthly active users. *Business Insider*. Retrieved from www.businessinsider.com/wechat-has-hit-1-billion-monthly-active-users-2018-3

Jiang, H., & Men, L. R. (2015). Creating an engaged workforce: The impact of authentic leadership, transparent communication, and work-life enrichment. *Communication Research*, *44*(2), 225–243. doi:10.1177/0093650215613137

Kang, J. H., Solomon, G. T., & Choi, D. Y. (2015). CEOs' leadership styles and managers' innovative behaviour: Investigation of intervening effects in an entrepreneurial context. *Journal of Management Studies*, *52*(4), 531–554.

Kuratko, D. F. (2007). Entrepreneurial leadership in the 21st century. *Journal of Leadership and Organizational Studies*, *13*(4), 1–11.

Lloyd, K. J., Boer, D., Keller, J. W., & Voelpel, S. (2015). Is my boss really listening to me? The impact of perceived supervisor listening on emotional exhaustion, turnover intention, and organizational citizenship behavior. *Journal of Business Ethics*, *130*, 509–524.

Luo, Y., Huang, Y., & Wang, S. L. (2011). Guanxi and organizational performance: A meta-analysis. *Management and Organization Review*, *8*(1), 139–172.

Macnamara, J. (2016). Organizational listening: Addressing a major gap in public relations theory and practice. *Journal of Public Relations Research*, *28*(3–4), 146–169. doi:10.1080/1062726X.2016.1228064

Mayfield, J., & Mayfield, M. (2017). Leadership communication: Reflecting, engaging, and innovating. *International Journal of Business Communication*, *54*(1), 3–11.

Mayfield, J., & Mayfield, M. (2018). *Motivating language theory: Effective leader talk in the workplace*. Cham: Palgrave Macmillan.

Men, L.R. (2015). The internal communication role of the Chief Executive Officer: Communication channels, style, and effectiveness. *Public Relations Review, 41*, 461–471. doi:10.1016/j.pubrev.2015.06.021

Men, L.R., & Bowen, S. (2017). *Excellence in internal communication management*. New York, NY: Business Expert Press.

Men, L.R., Chen, Z.F., & Ji, Y.G. (2018). Walking the talk: An exploratory examination of executive leadership communication at start-up companies in China. *Journal of Public Relations Research, 30*, 33–56. doi:10.1080/10627 26X.2018.1455147

Men, L.R., & Tsai, W.S. (2012). How companies cultivate relationships with publics on social network sites: Evidence from China and the United States. *Public Relations Review, 38*, 723–730.

Men, L.R., & Tsai, W.S. (2017). Authenticity. In B. Heath & W. Johansen (Eds.), *The international encyclopedia of strategic communication*. New York, NY: John Wiley & Sons, Inc.

Rawlins, B.L. (2009). Give the emperor a mirror: Toward developing a stakeholder measurement of organizational transparency. *Journal of Public Relations Research, 21*, 71–99.

Reis, H.T., Sheldon, K.M., Gable, S.L., Roscoe, J., & Ryan, R.M. (2000). Daily well-being: The role of autonomy, competence, and relatedness. *Personality and Social Psychology Bulletin, 26*(4), 419–435.

Renko, M., Tarabishy, A.E., Carsrud, A.M., & Brännback, M. (2015). Understanding and measuring entrepreneurial leadership style. *Journal of Small Business Management, 53*(1), 54–74.

Robinson, V.M. (2001). Embedding leadership in task performance. In K. Wong & C.W. Evers (Eds.), *Leadership for quality schooling* (pp. 90–102). New York, NY: Routledge/Falmer.

Rus, M., Ruzzier, M.K., & Ruzzier, M. (2018). Startup branding: Empirical evidence among Slovenian startups. *Managing Global Transitions, 16*(1), 79–94.

Ruvio, A., Rosenblatt, Z., & Hertz-Lazarowitz, R. (2010). Entrepreneurial leadership vision in nonprofit vs. for-profit organizations. *The Leadership Quarterly, 21*, 144–158.

Swiercz, P.M., & Lydon, S.R. (2002). Entrepreneurial leadership in high-tech firms: A field study. *Leadership & Organization Development Journal, 23*(7), 380–389.

Walumbwa, F.O., Avolio, B.J., Gardner, W.L., Wernsing, T.S., & Peterson, S.J. (2008, February). Authentic leadership: Development and validation of a theory-based measure. *Journal of Management, 34*, 89–126.

Xia, Y., & Mao, Y. (2016). Mobile phone usage in organizational communication and decision-making: Experience of employees in a multinational company's China branch. In I Management Association (Ed.), *Leadership and personnel management: Concepts, methodologies, tools, and applications* (pp. 1673–1689). doi:10.4018/978-1-4666-9624-2.ch074

8 Social media communication strategies for startups

The prevalent use of social media today has drastically changed the way businesses and stakeholders communicate. Undoubtedly, social media has been recognized as an integral component for businesses large and small, but the "how to" part remains a puzzle for many. A quick Google search "social media strategy for startups" has generated millions of results within a split second, showing different guides, tips, and cases. Naturally, given the restraint of resources, startups turn to social media for more cost-effective and targeted solutions. Intuitive as it may seem, there is no "one-size-fits-all" panacea. However, evidence-based best practices would help provide insights for startups to find the strategies that fit their own companies. This chapter draws insight from both theories and empirical studies regarding effective social media use for startups in China and provides practical recommendations for Chinese entrepreneurs and startups. We first review the characteristics of social media and the unique social media landscape in China. We then look at the purposes of social media communication for startups and discuss various social media communication strategies and tactics that can be adopted by Chinese startups and entrepreneurs.

Social media characteristics

Naturally, social media is about being "social," and the driving force is the people and communities behind the platforms. For example, marketing scholars Kaplan and Haenlein (2010) defined social media as Internet-based applications that "allow the creation and exchange of user-generated content" (p. 61). Public relations scholars Lariscy, Avery, Sweetser, and Howes (2009) defined social media as "online practices that utilize technology and enable people to share content, opinions, experiences, insights and media themselves" (p. 314). The power of social media comes from its capability to carry the content generated by both organizations and stakeholders, and to allow different parties of interests to engage and interact. As compared with traditional media channels (e.g., newspapers, TVs, email), social media has the following advantageous features.

Interactivity

Interactivity on social media is demonstrated in two ways. The first type, referred to as functional interactivity, is enabled by the functional features such as buttons to like and share, links to external sites, and the ability to make comments (Sundar, Kalyanaraman, & Brown, 2003). The other type of interactivity is message-based, known as contingency interactivity (Rafaeli, 1988). It highlights the feature of social media that allows the exchange of content and messages based on previous information transmissions.

Vividness

In addition to interactivity, social media also allows users to post multimedia content such as video, audio, and pictures, which enriches the sensory perception in a mediated environment that mimics real, in-person experience (Coyle & Thorson, 2001). This kind of sensory perception is known as *vividness*, which helps attract attention and increase the efficacy of information processing (Jiang & Benbasat, 2007).

Connectedness

Being social is being connected. Companies try to connect with their stakeholders. Individuals try to connect with their family, friends, and professional networks. The connectedness of social media results in various communities in which people get information they need from each other. Li and Bernoff (2008) referred to such social trend as the "groundswell movement," where people use technology to get what they need from each other, rather than from traditional institutions and corporations. People naturally trust the information provided to them by their communities and when there is no self-interest attached to that information. Although such needs existed long before the infancy of social media, technology today has made the trend much more prevalent with the ease to connect and exchange information.

Openness

Depending on the type of platforms, organizations and stakeholders are operating in an open or semi-open environment. Not only is the company-generated content for the world to see, but also is the feedback from individual users. The openness of social media allows word-of-mouth to be more readily available to multitude of audiences. Such openness brings both opportunities and challenges for companies. On the one hand, the scale of impact from positive word-of-mouth can be amplified, allowing third-party endorsement to reach beyond just one individual's network. On the other hand, the detrimental effect of negative word-of-mouth can also be enlarged, preventing potential customers from buying products and services or even triggering alerts for shareholders and investors.

As we review the characteristics of social media, one key thing to keep in mind is that technologies, platforms, and tools may change over time, but human needs to connect and communicate stay. Although some of the characteristics mentioned are related to technology features, it is the human needs that they all aim to address.

The current social media landscape in China

The social media landscape in China may appear different from the rest of the world. Due to Internet censorship from the government, many of the most popular social media platforms such as Facebook, Twitter, and YouTube are not accessible for Chinese users. However, that does not mean social media is used any less in China than the rest of the world. As of 2018, there were 673.5 million social media users in China, and this number is projected to grow to 799.6 million in 2023 (Statista, 2019). In the United States, that number is 243.6 million for users in 2018 and 257.4 million for projected users in 2023. As a collectivist society, people in China tend to rely on information shared by their own social networks. Social media, in this regard, has further fueled the capability for users to obtain and exchange information from one another. The report from the China Internet Network Information Center (CNNIC) in 2017 showed that consumers in China use social media for various activities, among which reading updates from friends/microblogs and sharing and forwarding information ranked the highest, followed by posting/updating status, and consuming video/audio content (CNNIC, 2017). As a result from the restriction on platforms such as Facebook, Twitter, and YouTube, and the need of information consumption and exchange from users, domestic social media platforms (e.g., Weibo, WeChat, QQ zone, Douyin [TikTok], Zhihu, Douban, and Xiaohongshu) have boomed in China over the years.

WeChat (Weixin)

WeChat was launched in 2011 by Tencent, one of the largest Chinese Internet companies. It was initially used as an instant messaging mobile application and known as the Chinese version of WhatsApp. In 2012, WeChat launched its "Moments" function, where users can post status updates via texts, photos, short videos, and shared links. The status is semi-public, which means users can choose to share the content only with their contacts or a selected group of contacts, and can only see the likes and comments from their own contacts under others' status updates. Companies can also set up their official accounts on WeChat, in which users can not only see published content but also interact with the company via in-app features. Moreover, WeChat continues growing its user base by incorporating different functions such as payment, ride sharing, and online shopping into the app (Chan, 2019).

Weibo

Weibo was launched in 2009 by the Internet giant Sina and has since grown into one of the most widely used social media platforms in China. As a microblogging site, Weibo embodies some quite distinctive features from Twitter. It allows richer media content and uses micro topics and a medal award system to encourage participation. Many companies turn to Weibo for information sharing and community building. In China, the number of microblogging users has witnessed a steady increase from 2010 to 2018. As of 2018, about 350.6 million people in China had used microblogging sites such as Weibo (CNNIC, 2018).

Other platforms

There are also many other social media platforms in China. QQ, another instant messaging app owned by Tencent, along with its blogging site QQ zone, is popular among teenagers and young adults. TikTok (Douyin), a short-form video app, has also been gaining momentum since its launch in 2016. In addition, there are also Dianping (a review site for services such as restaurants and bars that is known as the Chinese version of Yelp), Zhihu (a question and answer site that resembles Quora), Douban (content sharing site based on interests), Xiaohongshu ("Little Red Book," a product review and discussion site), and many others.

However, just like the social media landscape in Western countries, the specific usage of each platform in China is constantly changing, and new platforms are emerging. Therefore, the purpose of this section is to provide a background rather than a comprehensive list of these social media platforms. Startups in China should constantly follow up with the trend in social media usage and know where their stakeholders and audiences are.

Major purposes of social media communication for startups

For startups, the purposes of social media communication may be different from those of large, established companies. These purposes are closely associated with the specific characteristics of startups. Although startups do share with large companies on purposes of branding and reputation building, they also tend to focus on generating awareness of their offerings. From our interviews with 28 entrepreneurs in China, we found that startups mainly use social media to generate awareness and knowledge, boost word-of-mouth, cultivate long-term relationships, develop new businesses, and build brand image and corporate reputation (Chen, Ji, & Men, 2017).

Generating awareness and knowledge

Without established reputation and knowledge, startups first need to get their names known to survive. Creating awareness and knowledge thus becomes one of the most critical purposes of social media communication for startups. Just as Zhan, the CEO of an e-commerce startup put it, without awareness from the customers, the startup could not build its own brand. Ke, the CEO of a food manufacturing startup, further pointed out that having content ready on their WeChat official account also tells the investors who they are and what they do. It may sound intuitive that this purpose is usually tied with the tactic of frequent exposure, but too much repetition may become intrusive and counterproductive. Many high-tech startups thus turn to posting content about the industry in addition to about the companies themselves.

Boosting word-of-mouth

Related to the purpose of generating awareness and knowledge is the goal to encourage word-of-mouth and information sharing by current and potential customers. Social media is about social and user-generated content. For startups, having word-of-mouth and information sharing by their customers is a more effective way to "pull" in their target audience than merely having the company "push" the content to subscribers. Zhan, the CEO of an e-commerce startup, told us that word-of-mouth from their current customers helps attract prospects who are contacts of these customers, thus helping create a snowball effect. More importantly, word-of-mouth also carries the effects of third-party endorsement, where the information comes from a non-company-affiliated individual. Thus word-of-mouth not only helps startups increase their visibility, but the information shared is also more likely to be trusted.

Cultivating long-term relationships

Social media is about communities. To connect with communities, startups need to cultivate relationships with these communities for the long run. Such effort is manifested both in the relevance and value of content produced on social media, and in the feedback and customer service system. Hang, the CEO of a 3D home design startup, shared that his company builds and maintains long-term relationships with customers, prospects, and investors by constantly updating them with their new product features and tips for home décor on the company's Weibo and WeChat sites. In addition to this kind of proactive posting on social media, startups – especially those in the service industry – also take advantage of the interactive and two-way communication characteristics in their customer services. For example, Ke, the CEO of a food manufacturing startup, told us that his company takes customer feedback on social media seriously. When there were complaints about his company's food product quality, he chose to refund the unsatisfied customers. For Ke, the value of positive long-term relationships with customers far outweighed the refund's immediate impact on company revenue.

Developing new businesses

Intuitively, developing new businesses is also a significant purpose for startups' use of social media. Many hope the content would generate conversion and eventually sales revenue. For Yue, the CEO of a food manufacturing startup, good social media content can be directly related to his company's revenue. As they started embedding hyperlinks in the social content, they had noticed an increasing amount of traffic to the company's e-commerce site. For B2B startups, the hyperlinks in social media content may also turn into lead generation, as potential business customers try to send inquiries for quotes as they decide to adopt the product/service for their organizations.

Building brand image and corporate reputation

As startups get their names known and social media content shared, another purpose of their social media communication is to build brand image and corporate reputation. As part of the strategic communication efforts, startups' social media strategies should align with the type of image they want to initiate. Content should also match what the startup does to build a positive corporate reputation. As much effort as a startup wants to invest in creating attractive content, if it does not live up to what the company does, it will cause the opposite effect. Wu, the CEO of a startup focusing on control products and solutions for fluid machinery, told us:

> If your company doesn't even have a social media account, customers may not think your company is as legit. However, if your company has a great social media account, but people find out the company itself is quite underdeveloped, then still, there will be no way that they want to do business with you.

Startup social media communication strategies and tactics

To serve the social media communication purposes and meet goals and objectives, startups need to have effective social media strategies and tactics. In this chapter we provide several theory informed and research-based strategies and tactics as guidelines for startups.

Social media content strategies

Information dissemination and sharing

The strategy of information dissemination and sharing mainly serves the purpose of generating awareness and knowledge. Many of the entrepreneurs we interviewed told us that much of their social media content was information about the company, products, or services. Startups use social media as practical tools to inform their customers about new product launches, announce new venture investment funds, or strategic partnership with other companies. Our content analysis of 419 corporate social media posts on Weibo and WeChat by startups showed that 44.5% of the Weibo content and 34.2% of the WeChat content was about information dissemination. This in fact concurs with the need from consumers. Our recent survey with 1,066 social media users in China showed that 69.42% of the users surveyed indicated they were "somewhat interested," "interested," or "strongly interested" in learning about company-related information from startups on social media. Even more (88.28%) showed such interests in learning about information related to startups' products and services.

Promotion and mobilization

Promotional and mobilizing strategies are also commonly used by startups, especially for those that directly interact with consumers. Startups often use promotions and sales to attract their customers to follow, share, and make purchases. For example, an Internet-based beauty services startup based in Beijing once launched a social media campaign where customers could share a "red pocket" of 100 yuan as a monetary incentive to use their service in their own WeChat "moments." The "red pocket" would then be split randomly among eight people to use their beauty services. Ju, the COO of a mobile app that offers personal grocery shopping services, simply told us that customers loved sales and promotions. Indeed, the need for promotion and sales is high from consumers, as 77.77% of the 1,066 Chinese social media users in our survey said they were interested in content related to promotion and sales from startups on social media.

Social listening, customer service, and dialogue

Perhaps listening is the strategy that most capitalizes on the interactive, two-way communication, and community-focused characteristics of social media. Social listening and dialogue allow startups to engage their customers more directly, build communities, and resolve problems timely. Ping, the CEO of an Internet-based beauty services startup, told us that her company had a customer service team that monitors social media conversations. They would bring issues to the management team if they see potential red flags and resolve complaints in a timely fashion. Many entrepreneurs we interviewed also acknowledged that social listening, customer-service and dialogue determined whether the word-of-mouth their customers generate would be positive or negative. In line with what the entrepreneurs shared with us, engaging in social listening, dialogue, and online customer service is also what consumers expect from Chinese startups. From our survey, 69.24% of the 1,066 Chinese social media users indicated interests in content related to customer service and dialogue. Therefore, we recommend startups in China to acknowledge the importance of social listening, dialogue building, two-way communication, and taking full advantage of the interactive features of social media.

Thought leadership building

One of the unique social media communication strategies we found from our interviews with entrepreneurs was thought leadership building. This type of content may not be directly related to the company or its products but would include useful information related to the industry as a whole. This strategy is especially favored by B2B startups. Yuan, the CEO of a SaaS startup, remarked that in order to generate awareness and educate the market, his company posts many opinion pieces on social media to provoke thoughts and get more exposure in the tech community. Jie, the CEO of an education services startup, also mentioned that his company would post content about how-tos for it to be shared more widely. Concurring with what the entrepreneurs shared with us, consumers' interests in thought leadership–related content are also high, with 82.83% of those surveyed indicating interests in this type of content.

Co-branding and utilizing third-party endorsement from influencers

Because startups usually have limited resources and are yet to establish their corporate identity and reputation, many turn to the strategy of co-branding and influencer endorsement on social media to boost exposure. Yue, the

CEO of a food manufacturing startup, shared with us a social media campaign they implemented in collaboration with a more well-known transportation tech company to provide discounted transportation to the event held by his company. In that way, both companies got exposure to each other's customers. Many startups also turn to celebrities and influencers for endorsement. This strategy indeed helps generate more views and exposure, as indicated by our interviewee Zhan, the CEO of an e-commerce startup. However, celebrity endorsement is not always well received by consumers. Although 60.88% of consumers in our survey indicated interests in celebrity endorsement in startups' social media content, many commented that they did not want to see an endorsement from certain celebrities due to their tarnished reputation. Therefore, although co-branding and celebrity endorsement help boost exposure, startups need to take caution when adopting this strategy to avoid associations with certain negative reputation from the companies and celebrities they collaborate with.

Social media messaging tactics

Different from the overarching communication strategies, social media messaging tactics focus more on the specific delivery of information. Scholars in public relations and strategic communication suggested social media messages should carry appropriate message appeals, a conversational human voice, and incorporate the interactive and vivid platform features to generate effective outcomes (e.g., Chen et al., 2017; Men & Tsai, 2016).

Use appropriate message appeals

Startups may use different types of message appeals to engage their stakeholders. Commonly used message appeals in social media posts include emotional appeal (i.e., addressing the emotional aspects associated with a brand or product), informational appeal (i.e., presenting a product's quality and performance), and humor appeal. For example, Qing Song Chou, a crowdfunding startup in China that provides fundraising platforms for causes and medical bills, often uses emotional appeal in its social media messages (*Example*: 有一群孩子，他们渴望得到知识，但每天睁眼看到的都是白色的世界 😊# 上轻松筹，支持爱心病房图书馆# c *translation*: "There are a group of kids. They are eager to gain knowledge, but all they can see every day is a world covered in white [hospital bed sheets] [emoji of 'being sick'] #join Qing Song Chou to support hospital library for kids#").

Keep, a social fitness app startup in China, uses informational appeal to provide fitness tips (*Example*: 健身这回事，三分练七分吃，吃对食物很重要！健康餐 = 食草动物+万物水煮 的时代已经过去了，科学的健身美食栏目「Keep 食验室」，让你在迈开腿的时候，也能讨好嘴

– *translation*: "Fitness is 30% exercise and 70% diet, so eating the right food is very important. The era of 'healthy diet = vegetarian + everything boiled' is over. Our fitness cuisine program 'Keep kitchen' allows you to enjoy food while exercising"). They also use humor appeal to engage users with funny content (example: 独家秘方，百试百灵的减肥方法，亲测有效 [picture showing: 减肥的方法，先将头往右转，然后再往左转，当有人请你吃东西时，请重复这个动作] – translation "One of a kind evidence-proofed weight-loss method [picture showing: Weight-loss method, please turn your head to the right, then to the left. When someone asks you to eat, please repeat this movement]"). In addition, startups also use vision appeal to present an outlook toward the future. Vision appeal is often used with a startup's updates on their business development, innovation, and funding.

Incorporate conversational human voice and personification features

Social media communication is not about disseminating information in a one-way direction, but about engaging stakeholders. Kelleher (2009) suggested that conversational human voice in social media content would help generate more positive attitudinal, relational, and behavioral outcomes. For instance, Ant Financial (formerly known as Alipay), an Alibaba Group–affiliated Fintech unicorn, often uses a casual, conversational, and informal tone that includes salutations and inclusive pronouns (*Example*: 用技术保障消费 我们是认真的 – *translation*: "Using technology to protect consumption [rights] [🐜] We are being serious"). Such conversational human voice also fits well with its logo – an anthropomorphic ant. In our content analysis, results indeed showed conversational human voice was effective in generating more views, shares and/or comments on WeChat and Weibo. This effect is known to be driven by the potential of dialogic communication and personification via social media. The combination of conversational human voice and emojis could further enhance brand personification. As China is a high-context society in its cultural dimension (see more about Chinese culture in Chapters 2 and 6), companies tend to rely heavily on emojis to provide a more personable and relatable context of their messages on social media.

Take advantage of platform features

In our research, we found many startups take full advantage of the multimedia features of social media to enhance the interactivity and vividness of their content. However, startups need to be careful with overusing such features. The adoption of a site's interactive and vivid functions is helpful in generating more engagement (e.g., Coyle & Thorson, 2001; Guillory & Sundar, 2014). It is thus intuitive for startups to be compelled to use all functions of a social media platform. However, recent public relations and strategic communication research showed that utilizing too many functions may not necessarily be a good thing (e.g., Chen et al., 2017; Ji, Chen, Tao, & Li, 2019). Too many hashtags and hyperlinks may drive the traffic away, and too many emojis and pictures may also distract the audience from fully processing the central content. Therefore, while startups should take advantage of these features, they also need to be wary of the excessive use of such features. After all, they are tactics serving to implement the content strategy and should not overwhelm the central message and distract the audience from the primary purpose.

In summary, to have effective social media communication programs, startups should understand the interactive, vivid, open, and community-focused characteristics of social media and acknowledge that social media is not just about informing but about engagement. They also need to stay on top of the current social media landscape and trends in China and adjust their adoption of platforms when changes arise. Social media communication should not be regarded as isolated events or fragmented posts but should be integrated as part of the overarching strategic communication programs that take the whole strategic planning process. While information dissemination, promotion, and thought leadership need to be incorporated as part of startups' social media communication strategies, startups also need to further incorporate the social listening, customer-service and dialogue content strategies. Furthermore, as effective as celebrity endorsement may seem to be in generating awareness and exposure, startups need to be careful about choosing the celebrities or co-branding companies and evaluate the potential risks if the celebrity or collaborating company's reputation might be at risk. Finally, depending on the company's desired brand voice, startups should use appropriate message appeals, incorporate conversational human voice, and carefully leverage the interactive and vivid platform features. While this chapter provides some practical insights for startups' social media communications, it is important to note there's no one-size-fits-all approach. Each startup should develop its own social media communication programs with their communication needs, purposes, target audiences, and company features and culture in mind.

References

Bernoff, J., & Li, C. (2008). *Groundswell: Winning in a world transformed by social technologies*. Boston, MA: Harvard Business School Publishing.

Chan, J. (2019). All you need to know about the Chinese social media landscape in 2019. *Linkfluence*. Retrieved from www.linkfluence.com/blog/chinese-social-media-landscape-2019

Chen, Z. F., Ji, Y. G., & Men, L. R. (2017). Strategic use of social media for stakeholder engagement in startup companies in China. *International Journal of Strategic Communication, 11*(3), 244–267.

CNNIC. (2017, December 27). Leading activities of social network users in China as of 2016, by social network [Graph]. *Statista.* Retrieved on August 25, 2019 from www.statista.com/statistics/277655/china-social-network-most-frequent-activities-by-social-network/

CNNIC. (2019, February 28). Number of microblog users in China from December 2010 to December 2018 (in millions) [Graph]. *Statista.* Retrieved on September 1, 2019 from www.statista.com/statistics/321806/user-number-of-micro blogs-in-china/

Coyle, J. R., & Thorson, E. (2001). The effects of progressive levels of interactivity and vividness in web marketing sites. *Journal of Advertising, 30*(3), 65–77.

Grunig, J. E., & Hunt, T. T. (1984). *Managing public relations.* New York, NY: Holt, Rinehart and Winston.

Guillory, J. E., & Sundar, S. S. (2014). How does web site interactivity affect our perceptions of an organization? *Journal of Public Relations Research, 26*(1), 44–61.

Ji, Y. G., Chen, Z. F., Tao, W., & Li, Z. C. (2019). Functional and emotional traits of corporate social media message strategies: Behavioral insights from S&P 500 Facebook data. *Public Relations Review, 45*, 88–103.

Jiang, Z., & Benbasat, I. (2007). Research note: Investigating the influence of the functional mechanisms of online product presentations. *Information Systems Research, 18*(4), 454–470.

Kaplan, A. M., & Haenlein, M. (2010). Users of the world, unite! The challenges and opportunities of social media. *Business Horizons, 53*(1), 59–68.

Kelleher, T. (2009). Conversational voice, communicated commitment, and public relations outcomes in interactive online communication. *Journal of Communication, 59*(1), 172–188.

Lariscy, R. W., Avery, E. J., Sweetser, K. D., & Howes, P. (2009). An examination of the role of online social media in journalists' source mix. *Public Relations Review, 35*(3), 314–316.

Men, L. R., & Tsai, W.H.S. (2016). Public engagement with CEOs on social media: Motivations and relational outcomes. *Public Relations Review, 42*(5), 932–942.

Rafaeli, S. (1988). From new media to communication. *Sage Annual Review of Communication Research: Advancing Communication Science, 16*, 110–134.

Statista. (2019, February 18). Number of social network users in selected countries in 2018 and 2023 (in millions) [Graph]. *Statista.* Retrieved on August 25, 2019 from www.statista.com/statistics/278341/number-of-social-network-users-in-selected-countries/

Sundar, S. S., Kalyanaraman, S., & Brown, J. (2003). Explicating web site interactivity: Impression formation effects in political campaign sites. *Communication Research, 30*(1), 30–59.

9 Best practices of startup strategic communication

On June 13, 2019, China's Premier Li Keqiang visited Hangzhou, a vibrant and dynamic city nicknamed China's new Silicon Valley, where Jack Ma founded the Internet giant Alibaba 20 years ago. To encourage and facilitate startup economy, the municipal government of Hangzhou built the "Dream Town," a 3.47 km² incubator and entrepreneurial ecosystem built for high-tech and Internet startups in 2014 and located close to Alibaba's headquarters. In the "Dream Town," Premier Li delivered a speech for the 2019 Mass Entrepreneurship and Innovation Week, calling for further boosting mass entrepreneurship to stimulate market players' vitality and social creativity and strengthen new growth impetus. Within five years, with tremendous government support and benefits offered, such as training, rental subsidies, cash handouts, and shared resources, the Dream Town, referred to as "a fantasy island born with dreams" by people in Hangzhou, has attracted over 10,000 entrepreneurs.

Hangzhou is one exemplar of the major cities in China, which have been fostering mass entrepreneurship and innovation following the call from China's central government. The Dream Town is also a snapshot of what is happening in the entrepreneurial and venture capital circles in this vibrant economy. As recognized by many startup founders we interviewed, startups in China have welcomed their best era in the past decade. This is especially the case for those that are venture-backed and in the Internet and high-tech industry.

Our book is devoted to providing a research-based and theory-informed understanding of how strategic communication can be effectively carried out in or for startups in China, an enormous emerging market with unique social, political, economic, and cultural characteristics. In this chapter, we conclude the key insights discussed in the book and present a list of best practice recommendations drawing from firsthand research, theories, and successful cases for startup leaders, entrepreneurs, communication managers, and consultants in China and internationally.

Recognizing the importance of startup strategic communication and the opportunities and challenges

The argument that communication is not as important in the early stage of startups as the financial and production issues has been a common misconception among many startups. However, an increasing number of entrepreneurs in China today, especially among the younger generations, have recognized the critical role that communication plays in startup identity and brand building, customer acquisition, culture cultivation, and stakeholder relationship management, among others. As an entrepreneur remarked, "If you don't think about communication from the beginning, you have to pay the efforts several times more later."

With its unique characteristics distinct from large corporations, startup strategic communication bears its own opportunities and challenges. On the one hand, startups (in China and elsewhere) often lack existing internal structures and processes. They start with no established brand and identity and usually have little customer base. They are also often limited in financial and human resources and knowledge from prior market success. Furthermore, in the absence of reliable signals of product quality, such as advertising expenditures and branding, trusting the startup or constructing the young firm's reputation can be challenging for stakeholders (Petkova, Rindova, & Gupta, 2008). On the other hand, these characteristics can be double-edged swords that bring about unique opportunities for startups that are not visible at big corporations, such as flexibility, speed of reaction and decision-making, dynamics, a relatively informal environment, and more employee autonomy.

Understanding the functions of startup public relations and strategic communication

Many entrepreneurs lack a comprehensive understanding of what startup public relations or strategic communication entail unless their business is in the communication industry. Thus, they need to be educated regarding what communication really is and, more importantly, what their particular communication needs are. They will likely make startup communication priority high in the company only when entrepreneurs truly recognize what communication can do for their business. Previous literature and our research have revealed the key functions of startup public relations and strategic communication. These functions vary from establishing the startup identity, brand, and culture, building startup image and reputation, generating word-of-mouth, managing stakeholder relationships, identifying issues, and managing crises, to more micro-level roles of customer acquisition, fostering, and retention and employee communication, among others. As Heath (2005) noted, depending on the challenges organizations face, they can strategically prioritize some of their communication functions by investing considerably more time, budget, and personnel.

Building a strong startup identity, brand, and culture

The argument that startup strategic communication starts with building a strong corporate identity, brand, and culture appeared as a consensus among the entrepreneurs we interviewed. Corporate identity can be regarded as a company's internal part of the corporate brand (Rode & Vallaster, 2005). The process of building the startup identity, brand, and culture essentially answers the questions of who we are, what we believe in, where we are heading, and how we are distinct from others in the market, which all come down to strategic communication. Startups should create and articulate a compelling, inspiring, and motivating vision that energizes, binds together, and instills confidence in stakeholders about a promising future of the company and speaks to a meaningful purpose of the startup that is associated with the greater good of society.

Time and efforts should also be devoted to building a strong culture of the startup, which is aligned with its vision, identity, and strategy and rooted in the distinctiveness of the startup and often the startup founder's/ entrepreneur's character or personality. They should also bear in mind the broad societal and national culture the startup operates in. For instance, if a returnee from the Western countries would like to start a new business in China, he/she should be equipped with cultural sensitivity and fully aware how Chinese consumers, employees, media, and government are different from those in the Western world. Startups can consider constructing the following types of culture, which we found constructive and effective for new ventures in China in our research. These culture values include innovation (i.e., risk-taking, trial and error, valuing new ideas, being bold and adventurous, and daring to think wild and crazy), openness (i.e., transparency, open flow of information, feedback, and adaptability to change), inclusiveness and participation (i.e., listening, equality and diversity of ideas and perspectives, empowerment, and sharing), supportiveness and people orientation (i.e., caring, empathy, individualized support, harmony and relationship focus, and sensitivity to human feelings), competitiveness/ aggressiveness (i.e., high-performance orientation, outcome driven, emphasis on goal attainment, sense of urgency, and crisis awareness), and fun and joy (i.e., value of happiness, sense of humor, excitement, playfulness, and work-life balance).

Establishing a favorable startup reputation

A startup's reputation is referred to how its various stakeholders perceive the company. Rooted in stakeholders' direct and indirect experiences with the company, startup reputation is not only shaped by consumers who have used the startup's products/services but also by those who are talking about the company (i.e., word of mouth, online and offline). Word of mouth is a crucial trustworthy source of information for consumers, especially in a relationship-oriented collectivist society, such as China. Thus, startups should proactively and strategically generate positive word of mouth through strategic communication efforts, such as partnering with social influencers (e.g., Big V on Weibo) to create social buzz about the brand or developing incentive programs for consumers' word-of-mouth engagement. Nonetheless, the basis of word of mouth is high-quality products and services.

Gone are the days of "Good wine needs no bush" (酒香不怕巷子深). To attract talents, build investor and consumer trust, and compete for resources from the government and media attention, startups must build a favorable image and reputation early. Several recommendations emerged from our research that can help entrepreneurs embark on the journey of reputation building for the new venture.

1 *Enhance online visibility.* Having a well-designed website and social media pages can increase the credibility of the startups among consumers.
2 *Participate in symbolic activities,* such as attending industry trade shows and conventions, giving speeches at professional conferences, publishing white papers to build thought leadership, and educating consumers about the startup's new technology or the vision and capabilities of the founding team (Petkova et al., 2008). Such activities help create public awareness of the startup brand and gradually accumulate positive public perceptions of the company.
3 *Invest in human capital.* Hiring experts, industry thought leaders, and talents with a proven track record can enhance the prestige aspect of the startup human capital.
4 *Form relationships and strategic partnerships with prominent industry players.* For instance, partnering with a renowned venture capital (VC) firm can instill confidence in other stakeholders about the startup and enhance its reputation, as the VCs are known to be expert evaluators of startups. Forming a strategic alliance with a well-established and reputable firm can convey social status and recognition of the startup by third parties (Petkova et al., 2008).

Building long-term relationships with key startup stakeholders

Similar to startup reputation, which takes time to establish, stakeholder relationship cultivation for startups in China requires the practice of strategic communication from the startup leader and its communication personnel over time. From day one, regardless of whether the entrepreneur recognizes relationship building as a public relations function, they engage in such activities naturally. In a guanxi-oriented society, such as China, building relationships, networks, and connections is an essential component of business activities and communications, as relationships ultimately bring resources, opportunities, and other tangible (e.g., cost reduction) and intangible assets (e.g., reputation, information) for startups. For instance, consumers who trust and are happy with a startup can voluntarily say positive things about the startup to their family and friends or even defend the company when it faces criticism. Government officials are more willing to share information about related policies and government resources with entrepreneurs whom they have good relationships with. Particularly, for startups challenged with financial issues and personnel shortage, access to information, publicity, and positive word of mouth generated from quality relationships with stakeholders are cost-effective resources for the new ventures.

To build long-term, mutually beneficial relationships with key stakeholders (e.g., employees, customers, investors, media, government, and community), startups in China can consider the following theory-based and research-evidenced strategies.

1   *Provide access to stakeholders*, such as listing detailed contact information on the web page, utilizing the commenting feature on social media channels, and leaders practicing an open-door policy (access).
2   *Collect and address stakeholder feedback.* The emergence of new technologies, such as big data analytics, has provided organizations new ways to listen to stakeholders, although this does not replace traditional channels, such as one-on-one meeting with investors, focus groups with consumers, or employee surveys. Beyond gathering feedback from stakeholders, stakeholders' feedback that is taken seriously by startups, which sends a signal of respect and trust, is what truly matters for relationship building (feedback).
3   *Attend networking activities and events.* If startups do not put their faces out there, then knowing them is difficult for investors, partners, or potential employees. Attending networking events, such as cocktail parties, business meals with investors or partners, or group outings

with employees, are effective face-to-face opportunities to nurture relationships with startup stakeholders (networking).

4   *Strive for a win-win solution.* A relationship that lasts in the business world is one that is beneficial for all parties involved. Although the startup is making profits, are consumers benefiting from using the startup's products/services (e.g., making their life easier and better)? Will investors get returns from working with the startup? Will the local government benefit from the growth of the startup (e.g., corporate taxes, employment opportunities for the area)?

5   *Leverage personal relationships* that entrepreneurs, startup leaders, or employees have with other stakeholders. After all, guanxi and *renqing* can reduce business cost and get things done more easily in China (win-win).

6   *Communicate the vision and values* (情怀) *of the startup to people,* inside out, which fosters deeper understanding among stakeholders regarding why the startup exists, what it does, and where it is heading. Compelling visions and strong values convey the startup's character, shape its brand, and build credibility and trust among stakeholders (vision/values).

7   *Be authentic and genuine.* Deep fake in the social era has increased consumers' anxiety about what to trust. The lack of trust toward institutions has become a global issue. For startups, with limited visibility and credibility in the early stage of brand building, being truthful, authentic, and genuine is essential for gaining and accumulating trust from consumers, investors, or employees (authenticity).

8   *Empower and involve stakeholders.* Empowering stakeholders is giving them the autonomy to voice their opinions and involve them in the startup decision-making process. Valuing diverse perspectives and the encouragement of ideas breed innovation and send a message that stakeholders are valuable partners for the startup, which can enhance relationships (empowerment).

9   *Keep stakeholders informed and updated.* For certain stakeholders, especially for investors and employees, startups need to keep them informed and in the loop. Investors who placed confidence in the entrepreneurs and invested venture capital deserve to know how their money was spent, how the business is going, and the revenue status, among others. Startups need to take proactive steps to periodically update the investors. Employees should be the first to know about the startup decisions, news, or activities (proactive reporting).

10 *Show positivity in interactions and communications with stakeholders.* As an attitude and a relationship cultivation strategy, positivity is creating an optimistic atmosphere, showing goodwill, and striving

to make relationships fun, enjoyable, and gratifying for stakeholders (positivity).

Capitalizing on the advantageous features of social media

The development of social technologies has fundamentally changed the communication landscape for organizations. Recognizing the unique advantageous characteristics of social media, such as being inherently two-way, interactive, conversational, communal, multimedia, and relationship oriented, many startups and entrepreneurs have embarked on the journey of going "social," using the cost-effective features of social media communication.

To reach where the stakeholders and audiences are today, *whether* startups should utilize social media is *not* a question anymore. The question that remains is, *how* can startups effectively use social media for various communication purposes, such as creating product or brand awareness and visibility, generating word of mouth, building stakeholder relationships, enhancing brand image and reputation, and acquiring new customers/ developing new business?

Although this book does not intend to provide a one-size-fits-all solution for startup social media communication, we provide some research-based recommendations for startups to get started in the "social" game:

1 *Develop interesting, relevant, useful, and sharable content that tailors to the stakeholders' needs.* "Content is king." This rule applies to corporate communication of all sizes on social media. To increase the reach of the message, social media content of startups should be fun, relevant, informative, and useful enough for people to share in their personal network. It should also be visual, engaging, and captivating to be able to compete for attention and strike a bond.

2 *Engage in genuine conversations with customers and listen proactively.* As compared to a static web page or an old-fashioned customer service hotline, social media provides dynamic platforms that allow consumers of the startup to have direct, authentic conversations with the new venture. This process bears enormous potential in that social media are public (or semi-public) spaces where every party can participate, pose questions, and express concerns and startups can listen, gather feedback, and promptly address issues and complaints. As startups often lack budget in market research, social media listening and customer feedback can provide tools and information for entrepreneurs

to feel the market pulse in the early stage and gauge customer needs and wants.

Through social media monitoring and listening, entrepreneurs can also catch what goes wrong, make corrective decisions, and mitigate issues, which may later turn into a crisis if undressed. In addition, the personal features of social media (e.g., emojis, stickers) allow the startup to have a genuine voice and project a vivid character in the digital sphere. Be it cute, funny, cool, or calm, social visibility can help increase the credibility of the startup.

3   *Build thought leadership.* Thought leadership building on social media is perceived as an effective way for startups to "generate higher exposure, drive information sharing and word-of-mouth, and establish professional and positive images" (Chen et al., 2017, p. 254). Unlike big corporations, which often generate "white papers," opinion editorials, proprietary research, and policy documents, the responsibility of thought leadership building at startups largely falls on startup leaders, such as the CEO and/or the founders. Startup leaders can engage in a range of activities to build confidence from stakeholders in their domain specialty, skills, and expertise. For example, they can write blogs and columns, share personal opinions on industry news, give webinars, take grassroots media and We-media interviews, or share "how-to" content to educate the market about their product or service-related topics.

4   *Practice co-branding.* Startups can form strategic partnerships with established companies, other startups, celebrities, or social influencers/opinion leaders, such as Weibo Big Vs, to promote their brand, enhance visibility, attract new clients, and form relationships. The key is to identify a third party that can cast a positive light on the startup's brand, mutually benefit from the collaboration, and share a similar target audience profile.

5   *Optimize social media platforms and tools.* Among the social media platforms and apps popular in China, which ones should the startup go for or start with – Blog, Weibo, WeChat, Youku, Kuai Shou, TikTok, Ling Ying, or others? There is no easy answer, but the key is to go where the target audiences are. While Weibo and WeChat are dominant social platforms in China, each social media app has its own features. Startups should avoid blindly investing in every platform. Instead, they should strategically identify the demographic and psychographic characteristics of the target audience, set social media communication objectives, and determine the nature of the content (e.g., a short, fun music video or a storytelling article).

Entrepreneurs and startup leaders as communication agents

At startups, especially in the early stage of a new venture, the entrepreneur often plays an important role in fulfilling the strategic communication function. Entrepreneurs' character, personality, and decision-making not only define the DNA and culture of the startup; they are also expected to set up, communicate, and live the vision of the organization through their verbal and non-verbal behaviors. Baum and Locke's (2004) longitudinal study of 229 entrepreneur CEOs and 106 associates revealed that startups' communicated vision had a direct effect on venture growth. As such, leaders' communication of the startup vision is as important as the vision content alone. After all, a vision that only sits there without being shared and interpreted will not be able to motivate high venture performance or inspire people.

The startup leader as the communication agent also serves critical functions in promoting and advocating the brand to internal and external stakeholders, online and offline. Without a specialized communication team, startup leaders are often the direct representative of the organization and the spokesperson in front of the media. Thus, it is not a surprise to see more and more entrepreneurs invest in personal branding as the startup leaders' personal brand and reputation can help construct the startup brand recognition and equity. Likewise, the personal networks that entrepreneurs have established with various stakeholders (e.g., investors, government officials, journalists, suppliers, competitors, and partners) can become crucial resources for startup development.

Startup leaders are entrepreneurs, innovators, strategic thinkers, and decision-makers. They are also team builders, mentors, recruiters, and facilitators. Thus, entrepreneurs should recognize their communication role in every aspect, be equipped with a strategic public relations mindset when making business decisions, and acquire effective communication skills. Although various communication strategies may work for different purposes (e.g., to inform, connect, and engage), research has revealed a set of communication principles that startup leaders should stand by, such as transparency, authenticity, empathy, care, respect, dialogue, collaboration, empowerment, and inclusion.

Strategically manage communication programs at startups

All communication philosophies, mindsets, and principles need to come down to the ground, which are implemented via communication programs or campaigns. At the micro level, for startup communication programs to be successful, they need to be managed following a strategic process: research, objectives, programing, and evaluation, known as the ROPE model, which is a formula commonly applied by public relations professionals.

1   *Research.* To start with, startups should conduct research, formal or informal, to analyze the situation, understand the internal and external environment (i.e., strengths and weaknesses, what is in the environment that goes for or against you), diagnose communication problems (e.g., awareness, branding, or engagement), and better understand the target audience (e.g., demographics, psychographics, behavioral patterns, and media consumption habits). This process can also help set up a benchmark for the communication program. For instance, if the startup intends to increase brand awareness, then they would want to know what and how much is known about their brand now.

2   *Objectives.* Based on the data collected in the research stage, communication problems and issues can be identified and target audiences can be better segmented. Then, specific goals and objectives should be set up for the communication program. While the goal is an overarching outcome that the startup intends to accomplish (e.g., to increase brand awareness), the objectives need to be laid out in a specific manner, measurable, achievable, relevant, and time-bound. There are in general three types of communication objectives: informational (e.g., knowledge, awareness), motivational (e.g., beliefs, attitudes), and behavioral (e.g., behaviors), which should be tied to the goal of the communication program as well as the business objectives of the startup. For instance, an informational objective can be "to increase the number of customers in Guangdong province who are aware of the brand vision by 20% by the end of 2019."

3   *Programming.* Goals and objectives spell out the desired outcome of the communication program (i.e., what we are trying to achieve). Programming pertains to message planning and implementation, which addresses the question of how we can get there. Specific communication strategies and tactics need to be developed with the communication goals, objectives, and target audiences in mind. In addition to developing a robust message platform, startups need to select appropriate media to get the key messages across to target audiences via online or offline events, news release, advertising, broadcast interviews, or social media engagement.

4   *Evaluation.* No evaluation, no improvement. For a young business in particular, everything they do is a learning process. The step of evaluation serves the purpose of not only assessing whether or to what extent the communication goals and objectives have been achieved, but also evaluating what went right or wrong, what worked or did not work, which could inform future communication planning. Evaluation should

also be conducted on a continuous basis, before, during, and after the communication program is implemented. It creates a feedback loop that provides useful information for startups to evaluate its status quo and adjust strategies and tactics accordingly.

The challenge is, similar to those in big corporations, that some startup leaders do not see the value of research and data and often skip the research stage to jump directly to decision-making. However, without a thorough understanding of the situation, environment, competitors, and especially target audiences, the decision-making could be shortsighted and its success will depend upon pure luck.

Listening

To make informed decisions, startups need to practice listening from the very beginning. While startup founders or leaders often serve as an agent of listening, gathering information and feedback from various stakeholders should be developed as an organizational capability and practiced systematically at startups. Listening to customers or users can help startups refine their product features or services to better serve the market needs; listening to investors can bring in an outsider's perspective from who truly cares about the survival of the business; listening to employees helps empower people who work for the startup and breed innovation. Broader listening on social media can monitor the environment, gauge public sentiment toward the brand, and identify and mitigate issues when possible. While for startups, listening may not top the list of business priorities, startup leaders and entrepreneurs of the company should develop a keen sense of the environment, value any feedback, and take in the information strategically. Strategic listening does not mean that startups should trust every source or piece of information; instead, it is a systematic capability, or even a habit to gather information, tease out noise, and use the useful data to inform decisions. It is especially critical for startups as they often face enormous uncertainties and instability of the market. Being constantly informed through every touch point, they can stay alerted, be able to identify early opportunities, sense risks, and prepare for the downturn of the market or any other potential challenges.

Seeking specialized assistance from professional public relations firms or consultants when needed

Taking a do-it-yourself approach to strategic communication, especially in the early stage of the new venture, is often cost-effective for startups. However, there are occasions when external help from specialized communication firms or consultants is needed. For instance, when the startup has a major need, such as launching their product or facing a big crisis, seeking professional help would become necessary. After all, communication is a specialized profession. While startup leaders can act as important communication agents, they would need expert insights from public relations professionals to handle major communication issues.

In closure, startups and new ventures are crucial to economic development in a society. In modern China, the private sector now accounts for more than three-quarters of the economy, and its impact continues to expand (Atherton & Newman, 2018). With the development of the mass entrepreneurship and innovation movement and government support for new ventures, the number of startups in China is expected to continue to skyrocket. While it may not be realistic to expect entrepreneurs and startup leaders to be communication experts, they need to understand the importance of strategic communication for startup survival and development. They also need to be equipped with a strategic public relations mindset, understand their communication needs, and master relationship cultivation and communication skills to fulfill their internal and external communication needs. Strategic communication at startups entails a variety of activities serving various purposes (branding, culture creation, reputation management, stakeholder relationship building, customer acquisition, talent retention, etc.), which are intertwined with many other organizational functions. Like it or not, it is tied to the survival and growth of the new venture. It is not an either/or question now regarding communication investment – it is about the question of how: how can we practice effective strategic communication at startups in the unique cultural and social context of China? How can we unlock the power of communication to serve for the new venture success? We hope our book has provided you some research-based and theory-informed insights to embark on the journey of startup strategic communication.

References

Atherton, A. M., & Newman, A. (2017). *Entrepreneurship in China: The emergence of the private sector*. London: Routledge.

Baum, J. R., & Locke, E. A. (2004). The relationship of entrepreneurial traits, skill, and motivation to subsequent venture growth. *Journal of Applied Psychology, 89*(4), 587–598.

Chen, Z. F., Ji, Y. G., & Men, L. R. (2017). Strategic use of social media for stakeholder engagement in startup companies in China. *International Journal of Strategic Communication, 11*(3), 244–267.

Heath, R. L. (2005). Functions of public relations. In R. L. Heath (Ed.), *Encyclopedia of public relations* (pp. 350–353). Thousand Oaks, CA: Sage.

Petkova, A. P., Rindova, V. P., & Gupta, A. K. (2008). How can new ventures build reputation? An exploratory study. *Corporate Reputation Review, 11*(4), 320–334.

Rode, V., & Vallaster, C. (2005). Corporate branding for startups: The crucial role of entrepreneurs. *Corporate Reputation Review, 8*(2), 121–136.

Index

Printed in the United States
by Baker & Taylor Publisher Services